Quantitative Methods

Mathematics for Business

4th edition

Mark Cleary, Anglia Ruskin University London

Jas Naidoo, Anglia Ruskin University London

© Mark Cleary and Jas Naidoo, under exclusive licence to Springer Nature Limited 2019

All rights reserved. No reproduction, copy or transmission of this publication may be made without written permission.

No portion of this publication may be reproduced, copied or transmitted save with written permission or in accordance with the provisions of the Copyright, Designs and Patents Act 1988, or under the terms of any licence permitting limited copying issued by the Copyright Licensing Agency, Saffron House, 6–10 Kirby Street, London EC1N 8TS.

Any person who does any unauthorized act in relation to this publication may be liable to criminal prosecution and civil claims for damages.

The authors have asserted their rights to be identified as the authors of this work in accordance with the Copyright, Designs and Patents Act 1988.

This edition published 2019 by

RED GLOBE PRESS

Previous editions published by British University Press

Red Globe Press in the UK is an imprint of Springer Nature Limited, registered in England, company number 785998, of 4 Crinan Street, London, N1 9XW.

Red Globe Press® is a registered trademark in the United States, the United Kingdom, Europe and other countries.

ISBN 978-1-352-00788-6 paperback

This book is printed on paper suitable for recycling and made from fully managed and sustained forest sources. Logging, pulping and manufacturing processes are expected to conform to the environmental regulations of the country of origin.

A catalogue record for this book is available from the British Library.

A catalog record for this book is available from the Library of Congress.

Contents

Acknowledgements		vi
Introduction		**1**
Why quantitative methods?		1
How to use this book		1
1	**Arithmetic operations and rounding**	**3**
1.1	Introduction	3
1.2	Rounding	3
1.3	Addition	5
1.4	Subtraction	7
1.5	Multiplication	9
1.6	Division	10
1.7	Integers, rounding and significant numbers	11
1.8	BODMAS	13
1.9	Review questions	16
1.10	Progress questions	20
2	**Fractions**	**22**
2.1	Introduction to fractions	22
2.2	Fractions in their simplest form	25
2.3	Addition and subtraction of fractions	27
2.4	Multiplication and division of fractions	30
2.5	Review questions	33
2.6	Progress questions	35
3	**Decimals**	**37**
3.1	Introduction to decimals	37
3.2	Rounding decimals	39
3.3	Converting fractions to decimals and decimals to fractions	40
3.4	Ratios	40

		3.5	Percentages	43
		3.6	Review questions	49
		3.7	Progress questions	52
4	**Test your knowledge**			**54**
		4.1	Paper 1	54
		4.2	Paper 1 answers	57
		4.3	Paper 2	60
5	**Wages, salaries, taxes, depreciation, commission and discounts**			**63**
		5.1	Introduction	63
		5.2	Wages and salaries	63
		5.3	Taxes	65
		5.4	Depreciation	67
		5.5	Commission	68
		5.6	Discounts	69
		5.7	Review questions	70
		5.8	Progress questions	73
6	**Interest calculations and foreign exchange**			**75**
		6.1	Introduction	75
		6.2	Simple interest and compound interest	75
		6.3	Foreign exchange	78
		6.4	Review questions	80
		6.5	Progress questions	81
7	**Test your knowledge**			**83**
		7.1	Paper 3	83
		7.2	Paper 3 answers	85
		7.3	Paper 4	88
8	**Tables, graphs and diagrams**			**91**
		8.1	Introduction	91
		8.2	Tables	91
		8.3	Graphs	99

	8.4	Diagrams	101
	8.5	Review questions	106
	8.6	Progress questions	114

9 Creating information and measures of centrality — 115

	9.1	Introduction	115
	9.2	Information	115
	9.3	Introducing the three measures of centrality	119
	9.4	Strengths and weaknesses of the measures of centrality	122
	9.5	Review questions	125
	9.6	Progress questions	128

10 Test your knowledge — 130

	10.1	Paper 5	130
	10.2	Paper 5 answers	132
	10.3	Paper 6	136

11 Drawing charts using Excel — 138

12 Answers to practice questions — 144

Acknowledgements

The authors would like to thank their students and colleagues who have provided them with feedback on the material in this book. They would also like to thank Aaron and Kieran Naidoo, whose work and ideas helped both Jas and Mark to produce a better book than they would have otherwise produced. Of course, despite this wonderful help and advice all errors remain the unfortunate property of the authors.

Introduction

Why quantitative methods?

Various studies undertaken by large supranational bodies and employers' federations have suggest that, unfortunately, many people lack the basic numerical skills that are required for work.

It is suggested by many that maths is just another academic area that a student needs to get through. But numeracy in business is essential. It is the language of commerce. We need basic mathematical skills in order to work out prices, costs, profits, taxes, discounts, wages and salaries!

We put an exclamation mark next to the last paragraph, because even if you don't want to know anything else about maths surely you want to know whether you are being paid correctly, that you are paying the right tax and what, if any wage increase, you could demand from your employer, or even what you should be paying your employees.

How to use this book

For some of you this book will be like a walk down Memory Lane where you will revisit long-distant faces from your past. In this case, the faces will be the mathematical symbols of your childhood and maybe the fear or anxiety that they brought you. However, there is no need to worry about that here because everything in this book assumes no prior knowledge. It starts from the very beginning and builds.

Maths isn't just about learning facts and techniques, it is about doing – solving problems – which should make its study enjoyable because it is interactive and often challenging.

In order to encourage interactive learning, there are four types of questions in this book. The first type are the Practice questions which are embedded within each chapter. They are designed to support and reinforce your learning, using examples and techniques that have just been covered within the text. You should always attempt these and then check your results against the answers at the back of the book.

Then there are two sets of questions at the end of the chapter: Review questions and Progress questions. Both types deal with the content you have studied within the chapter, so these questions cover all the topics and techniques required by you as the student and once again are designed to reinforce your learning. While there are answers to the Review questions, given immediately after the questions, there are no answers for the Progress questions because they may be set by your lecturers as homework.

The fourth type of question is embedded within the Test Your Knowledge sections. These tests are quite comprehensive and each test will take about an hour to complete. As with end-of-chapter questions, each Test Your Knowledge section has two tests. The first test has answers and is designed to be used by students to check their knowledge, while the second test is designed to be used in an examination situation. Tutors may set these as mock exams for their students.

Please note that you must follow the book in the order presented because some chapters assume that you have prior knowledge from previous chapters.

Finally, Chapter 11 – Drawing charts using Excel – is a new addition to this book and will, hopefully, be useful for students who want to extend their knowledge.

Good luck with your studies.

Jas and Mark

Chapter 1
Arithmetic operations and rounding

1.1 Introduction
1.2 Rounding numbers
1.3 Addition
1.4 Subtraction
1.5 Multiplication
1.6 Division
1.7 Integers, rounding and significant numbers
1.8 BODMAS
1.9 Review questions
1.10 Progress questions

1.1 Introduction

This chapter will deal with rounding and mathematical operations. In your early days at school you are likely to have come across many different symbols which you may well be familiar with. This chapter will revise these symbols and the mathematical operations associated with them and bring them together with a technique to deal with mixed operations called BODMAS. Although you will have the use of a calculator, it is good practice to do the calculations manually to grasp the methodology.

1.2 Rounding numbers

Every number is unique. Precision in numeracy is necessary, but on occasion it is acceptable to approximate, e.g. when asking how far it is to the nearest shop in the countryside, you may be told that it is 6 or 7 miles away.

Figures can be rounded up or rounded down when fine detail is not required. The rule that is applied when rounding numbers which are 5 or greater, 7 for instance, is that the figure is rounded up. Numbers that are 4 or smaller, 2 for instance, are rounded down.

We can round numbers to the nearest units, tens, hundredths and so on depending upon the exercise we are carrying out. These different roundings are known as rounding to a place value, although we usually just talk about rounding to the nearest number of some magnitude.

Figure 1.1 Place values

Rounding to the nearest ten

To illustrate this, we can look at rounding numbers to the nearest ten. If you are rounding 12 to the nearest ten, the last digit (the units) is examined. The tens column is rounded up if the last unit digit is 5 and over and rounded down if the unit digit is 4 and below.

Examples

When rounding to the nearest ten:

Number	Answer	Reasoning
12	10	The last digit is 2, so you round down
16	20	The last digit is 6, so you round up
25	30	The last digit is 5, so you round up

Rounding to the nearest hundred

When rounding to the nearest hundred, the same rule applies, i.e. half of a hundred is 50, so 50 (5 in the tens column) and above is rounded up, and 40 (4 in the tens column) and below is rounded down. Note that we ignore the numbers to the right of this rounded answer and simply place zeros to the right.

Examples

When rounding to the nearest hundred:

Number	Answer	Reasoning
734	700	3 is less than 5, so you round down
851	900	5, so you round up
1,321	1,300	2 is less than 5, so you round down

The same principles apply when rounding for thousands and millions.

Practice questions 1

1. Round off the following figures to the nearest ten:
   (a) 39
   (b) 63
   (c) 74
   (d) 91

2. Round off the following figures to the nearest hundred:
   (a) 369
   (b) 478
   (c) 249
   (d) 319

3. Round off the following figures to the nearest thousand:
   (a) 3,679
   (b) 46,823
   (c) 5,492
   (d) 7,381

4. Round off the following figures to the nearest million:
   (a) 3,292,167
   (b) 8,432,921
   (c) 9,674,943
   (d) 11,492,931

Now check your answers.

1.3 Addition (+)

This is indicated as a + sign. In attempting to add numbers the figures must be laid out in columns. This allows us to see clearly the units, tens etc. Effectively the presentation should follow the place value figure presentation in Figure 1.1 (repeated from above).

| Ten thousand(s) | Thousands | Hundreds | Tens | Units |

Figure 1.1 Place values

So, in attempting to add the numbers 29, 343, 69, 8,721, 3, 242 and 839, the presentation should look as follows:

```
    29
   343
    69
 8,721
     3
   242
   839
_____
10,246   Total
```

In terms of order of addition, the figures on the extreme right, the units, need to be added together first. In this case the total for the units column comes to 36, i.e. 3 tens and 6 units.

The last number from this sum is then placed in the units column of the totals area as it is six units. The 3 is a tens place and therefore needs to be added with all the tens in the tens column when this column is added up. We call this process 'carrying over', as in carrying over the tens to the tens column. Moving from the extreme right to the left, each column should be added sequentially one at a time. This procedure is continued until the calculation is completed. So, for the next column, the tens column 3 is added with all the other tens to provide an answer of 24, this is of course 24 tens. The 4 is placed in the tens column total area and the 2 is carried over to the hundreds column, to be added with all the other hundreds. The next step is to add the hundreds, which in this case also includes the 2 from the tens calculation. This provides an answer of 22 hundreds. The last figure 2 is placed in the hundreds column in the totals area and the other figure 2 is carried over to the thousands column. This provides an answer of 10; the 0 is placed in the thousands column in the totals area while the 1 is carried over to the tens of thousands column.

It is important to be able to check answers, and often in the workplace you must prepare simple tables to summarise data. These tables comprise a two-dimensional presentation of data in a column and row format, as in Table 1.1. Rows go across a table and columns go vertically up and down a table.

A	*B*	*C*	*D*	*E*	Total	
341	821	1,531	361	321	3,375	
729	1,321	649	43	168	2,910	
624	629	711	172	72	2,208	
39	718	822	147	191	1,917	
1,733	3,489	3,713	723	752	10,410	*Grand total*

Table 1.1 Simple table

When you add up all the rows or all the columns in Table 1.1, the total should be 10,410, which is a cross check.

Practice questions 2

Add up the rows and columns, and cross check your answers:

(a)	(b)	(c)	(d)	Total
964	17,201	369	639	
328	34	482	1,291	
792	931	79	421	
236	1,074	3,121	829	

1.4 Subtraction (–)

As with addition it is imperative to be neat and use the columns correctly. To subtract 243 from 659, the first point is to ensure that the figures are set out properly, as follows:

```
 659
-243
 ---
 416
```

In subtraction, it is possible to find that the digit being subtracted is in fact greater than the digit it is being subtracted from (see below example). In this case it is necessary to "borrow" one from the next column.

Example

```
 88
-79
 ---    Total
 ---
```

Here the 9 is obviously larger than the 8, so we borrow one ten from the tens column so the calculation now looks like this:

```
 87¹8
- 7 9
 ----
```

Here the 8 tens have been reduced to 7 tens and the other ten is being borrowed by the units column, so there are now temporarily 18 units in the units column.

continued overleaf

Now we can do the operation, units first 18 − 9 = 9; the answer goes in the units column in the totals area.

$$\begin{array}{r} 7^18 \\ -7\ 9 \\ \hline 9 \end{array}$$

Then we subtract 7 in the tens column from 7 in the tens column in the row above: 7 − 7 = 0

$$\begin{array}{r} 7^18 \\ -7\ 9 \\ \hline 0\ 9 \end{array}$$

Therefore, the answer is 9 overall.

Example

$$\begin{array}{r} 931 \\ -745 \\ \hline \end{array}$$

In this example 1 is smaller than 5, so 1 is borrowed from the next column, making the units in the unit column temporarily 11 (1 + 10). Therefore, we can now subtract the 5 from the 11 which gives 6 in the totals area and the tens units has been reduced by one ten to 2.

$$\begin{array}{r} 932^11 \\ -7\ 4\ 5 \\ \hline 6 \end{array}$$

Now it is the turn of the tens column. In this case it is 4 tens that need to be taken away from 2 tens, and to do this one hundred unit must be borrowed from the hundreds column and temporarily stored in the tens column.

$$\begin{array}{r} 9 8 3^1 2^1 1 \\ -\ 7\ 4\ 5 \\ \hline 8\ 6 \end{array}$$

So now the 4 can be taken away from the 12 to provide 8. Finally, for the hundreds column it is 8 hundreds take away 7 hundreds which leaves 1 hundred unit.

Therefore, the result is

$$\begin{array}{r} 9 8 3^1 2^1 1 \\ -\ 7\ 4\ 5 \\ \hline 1\ 8\ 6 \end{array}$$

Practice questions 3

Perform these subtractions:

(a) 349
    −271
    ‾‾‾

(b) 924
    −716
    ‾‾‾

(c) 1,126
    − 379
    ‾‾‾‾

1.5 Multiplication (×)

Multiplication can be thought of as repeated addition. So, for instance 42 × 2 is the same as adding 2 lots of 42 together which will produce a result of 84. The result of multiplication is usually known as the product. In multiplication problems there are two parts: the multiplicand and the multiplier. The multiplicand is the number to be multiplied by the multiplier; it is usually but not always written first. So, in the example we just looked at the multiplicand is 42 and the multiplier 2.

Example

356 × 17 = 6,052

The number to be multiplied – the multiplicand – is 356, while the multiplier is 17. The product is 6,052.

When dealing with larger figures column alignment is essential to engage in something called long multiplication. When you do this manually there are certain rules that you must follow, that is, the rules of long multiplication.

As in the other mathematical operations we have looked at, calculations must be undertaken sequentially with regard to the columns from right to left.

Example

```
    496
×    12
```

The first calculation is to multiply the multiplicand by the units number of the multiplier (496 × 2) which is 992, the number 2 represents the number of units. The 992 is placed on the first line in the answer area (see below). The next step is to multiply the multiplicand by the next number of the multiplier (which in this case represents tens and is 1). It is important to note that when multiplying by ten, you need to add a zero into the units column on the second line in the answer area; if multiplying by hundreds, two zeros on the third line in the answer area and so on.

So, in this case the first thing to insert on the second line of the answer area is a zero, then the product of 1 × 496, giving 4,960.

The final step is to add together these products in the answer area:

```
      496
×      12
      992
+4,960
    5,952
```

Practice questions 4

Multiply the following:

(a)   743
     × 21

(b)   641
     × 39

(c)   3,216
     × 254

1.6 Division (÷)

There are three terms that are used for division:

The number to be divided is the dividend.
The number that is to be divided into the dividend is the divisor.
The answer is the quotient.

Example

36 ÷ 4 = 9 where

36 (Dividend) ÷ 4 (Divisor) = 9 (Quotient)

The presentation indicating the requirement for division of this example could be shown in numerous ways, e.g.

36 ÷ 4   36/4 $\frac{36}{4}$

Practice questions 5

Divide the following:
(a) 1,581 ÷ 17
(b) 15,792 ÷ 21
(c) 139,584 ÷ 16

1.7 Integers, rounding and significant numbers

Quite simply, integers are whole numbers. Examples are 6, 9, 15, 21 and 32 and so on. Any numbers that are not whole, cannot be integers.

Examples of numbers that are not integers are $\frac{1}{2}$, $\frac{3}{8}$, $\frac{7}{9}$, 0.25, 0.93, 1.7 and 6.9.

By rounding up or down to the nearest whole number, a number becomes an integer.

Positive and negative numbers

In order to explain this operation, it is easiest to illustrate by using a scale known as the number line. Numbers to the left of zero are negative numbers while those to the right of zero are positive numbers.

Figure 1.2 The number line

Positive numbers

Visualise the scale. If 2 and 3 were added, it would be illustrated as follows:

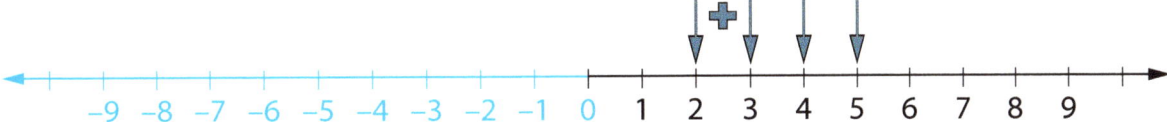

Figure 1.3 The number line, 2 + 3

The answer, as can be seen in Figure 1.3, is 5.

If the calculation was 5 + 3, the answer which is 8, could be illustrated as in Figure 1.4.

Figure 1.4 The number line, 5 + 3

Negative numbers

A negative number is less than zero. An example of this is a bank overdraft.

If I have a balance of zero in my bank account and I withdraw £30, my bank balance is overdrawn at –£30. This is a negative number.

There are certain rules that need to be applied when dealing with signs in negative number operations. These are:

> A plus and a minus result in a minus
>
> A minus and a minus result in a plus

To simplify calculations, it is often useful to use brackets, especially if you are unused to dealing with these types of numbers.

Example

+ 5 – 3

can be written as 5 + (–3).

The minus three (–3) is put in brackets to aid calculation later.

This effectively means that when a plus and a minus are added together the result is a minus away from the positive.

Therefore 5 – 3 = 2

Example

7 + (–8) =

7 – 8 = –1

At the beginning of this section on negative numbers I had a bank overdraft of £30. So, my bank account shows a balance of –£30. If I now withdraw another £50, my bank balance will be:

–£30 – (+£50) = –£80

Examples

(a) 5 − (−3) =

   The two minuses effectively cancel against each other and they become a positive:

   5 + 3 = 8

(b) 15 − (−6) =

   15 + 6 = 21

Practice questions 6

Work out the following:

(a) 5 + (−1)
(b) (−8) + 15
(c) 7 − (−5)
(d) 13 + (−17)
(e) (−16) + 4
(f) (−14) − (−3)
(g) (−9) + (−6)

1.8 BODMAS

Many calculations are complicated, with different mathematical operations needing to be undertaken in one calculation. To ensure that correct answer is calculated, it is necessary to perform the operations in a particular order. One way to remember the order of operations is to use the simple mnemonic **BODMAS**, which represents the mathematical order of priority of operations:

   Brackets
   Orders – powers and roots
   Division
   Multiplication
   Addition
   Subtraction

The order of operations is:

   Brackets What is inside brackets is calculated first. There may be more than one set of brackets in a calculation, in which case the contents of the inner bracket are calculated first, then the operations in the outer bracket.

   Orders Any power or root calculations are undertaken next.

   Division and Multiplication Then division and multiplication.

   Addition and Subtraction Finally, any additions and subtractions are calculated.

Brackets

Any calculations encapsulated within brackets must be calculated first.

Example

$(12 + 3) + (17 - 2)$

becomes

$15 + 15 = 30$

In terms of inner brackets as represented by [ ], the order of operations dictates that these come before all other calculations including round brackets ( ).

Example

$(12 + 3) + (1 + [14 - 4])$

$= (12 + 3) + (1 + 10)$

$= 15 + 11$

$= 26$

Orders

Powers and roots next.

Example

$3^2 \times (4 - 3)$

becomes

$3^2 \times 1$

$= 9 \times 1$

$= 9$

Example

$\sqrt{25} + 10 \times 5$

$= 5 + 10 \times 5$

$= 5 + 50$

$= 55$

Division and Multiplication

These calculations come after the brackets and roots and powers.

Example

$(7 + 9) \times 6$

$= 16 \times 6$

$= 96$

The brackets were calculated first, and then the multiplication.

Example

Bringing division into the previous example:

$(7 + 9) \times 6 \div 12$

$= 16 \times 6 \div 12$

$= 96 \div 12$

$= 8$

Addition and Subtraction

Example

$(7 + 9) \times 6 \div 12 + 7 - 2$

$= 16 \times 6 \div 12 + 7 - 2$

$= 96 \div 12 + 7 - 2$

$= 8 + 7 - 2$

$= 15 - 2$

$= 13$

Practice questions 7

(a) $(7 + 4) \times 3 + 2$
(b) $(7 + 4) \times (3 + 7)$
(c) $14 \times (6 + 3) - (15 \div 3)$
(d) $36 + 36 \div (3 \times 1)$
(e) $7 \times (48 \div [2 \times 2])$
(f) $(16 \div [3 + 1] + 8 + [3 \times 1] \times 6) \div 5$

1.9 Review questions

1. Round off the following figures.

   To the nearest ten:
   (a) 111 ; 55 ; 64 ; 33 ; 51
   (b) 249 ; 1 ; 14 ; 78 ; 100
   (c) 899 ; 34 ; 62 ; 74 ; 1,000
   (d) 12 ; 47 ; 85 ; 77 ; 43
   (e) 0 ; 6 ; 41 ; 115 ; 71

   To the nearest hundred:
   (a) 475 ; 879 ; 409 ; 1,059 ; 444
   (b) 320 ; 666 ; 41 ; 99 ; 750
   (c) 13 ; 589 ; 674 ; 888 ; 999
   (d) 114 ; 831 ; 900 ; 622 ; 847
   (e) 0 ; 149 ; 560 ; 134 ; 777

   To the nearest thousand:
   (a) 7,893 ; 3,748 ; 4,444 ; 1,400
   (b) 500 ; 9,311 ; 6,767 ; 2,689
   (c) 499 ; 99,899 ; 45,322 ; 5,500 ; 49,499
   (d) 3,123 ; 78,429 ; 7,938 ; 14,500 ; 9,657
   (e) 8,342 ; 12,576 ; 333 ; 0 ; 9,999

   To the nearest million:
   (a) 5,843,339 ; 16,937,859 ; 10,003,569 ; 2,485,359 ; 1,500,000
   (b) 499,999 ; 568,385,290 ; 6,792,475 ; 1 ; 79,249,273
   (c) 99,999,999 ; 567,000 ; 5,292,476 ; 56,873,000 ; 123,456,789
   (d) 0 ; 78,900,468 ; 100,000,000 ; 1,389,100 ; 6,666,666
   (e) 85,999,345 ; 34,333,333 ; 67,000,999 ; 67,999,000 ; 14,890,000

2. Add up the following rows and columns, and cross-check your answers.

   (a)

A	B	C	D	E	Total
567	901	631	276	440	
980	345	342	471	890	
5,123	12	789	4,590	78	
729	500	4,900	26	1,789	
678	14,789	470	134	2,300	

(b)

	A	B	C	D	E	Total
	476	888	123	957	100	
	347	540	321	890	580	
	7,469	97	110	1,923	145	
	345	913	7,800	71	12,309	
	789	9,560	900	651	1,000	

(c)

	A	B	C	D	E	Total
	999	34	89	276	120	
	679	934	503	846	456	
	6,320	57	765	3,123	52	
	789	10	1,700	7	2,690	
	900	15,900	550	678	7,800	

3 Subtract the following:

$$7{,}457 - 276 \qquad 321 - 41 \qquad 789 - 645 \qquad 7{,}821 - 74 \qquad 567 - 439 \qquad 730 - 399$$

4 Multiply the following:

$$371 \times 43 \qquad 429 \times 92 \qquad 631 \times 71 \qquad 492 \times 83 \qquad 671 \times 74$$

$$693 \times 21 \qquad 391 \times 84 \qquad 733 \times 21 \qquad 642 \times 33 \qquad 711 \times 11$$

5 Divide the following:
  (a) $1{,}463 \div 77$
  (b) $310{,}044 \div 84$
  (c) $44{,}098 \div 17$
  (d) $95{,}525 \div 25$
  (e) $221{,}766 \div 23$
  (f) $177{,}194 \div 19$
  (g) $38{,}505 \div 15$
  (h) $264{,}357 \div 27$

6 Calculate the following mixed options:
  (a) $(12 + 6) \times 7 + 3$
  (b) $(22 - 6) \times (7 + 1)$
  (c) $17 \times (19 + 5) - (33 \div 3)$

(d) 77 + 77 ÷ (9 + 2)
(e) 9 × (121 ÷ [97 − 86])
(f) 17 × 8 ÷ (23 − 15)
(g) (80 ÷ [9 + 1] + 4 + [3 × 6] × 6) ÷ 5

Answers

1   To the nearest ten:
   (a) 110 ; 60 ; 60 ; 30 ; 50
   (b) 250 ; 0 ; 10 ; 80 ; 100
   (c) 900 ; 30 ; 60 ; 70 ; 1,000
   (d) 10 ; 50 ; 90 ; 80 ; 40
   (e) 0 ; 10 ; 40 ; 120 ; 70

   To the nearest hundred:
   (a) 500 ; 900 ; 400 ; 1,100 ; 400
   (b) 300 ; 700 ; 0 ; 100 ; 800
   (c) 0 ; 600 ; 700 ; 900 ; 1,000
   (d) 100 ; 800 ; 900 ; 600 ; 800
   (e) 0 ; 100 ; 600 ; 100 ; 800

   To the nearest thousand:
   (a) 8,000 ; 4,000 ; 4,000 ; 1,000
   (b) 1,000 ; 9,000 ; 7,000 ; 3,000
   (c) 0 ; 100,000 ; 45,000 ; 6,000 ; 49,000
   (d) 3,000 ; 78,000 ; 8,000 ; 15,000 ; 10,000
   (e) 8,000 ; 13,000 ; 0 ; 0 ; 10,000

   To the nearest million:
   (a) 6,000,000 ; 17,000,000 ; 10,000,000 ; 2,000,000 ; 2,000,000
   (b) 0 ; 568,000,000 ; 7,000,000 ; 0 ; 79,000,000
   (c) 100,000,000 ; 1,000,000 ; 5,000,000 ; 57,000,000 ; 123,000,000
   (d) 0 ; 79,000,000 ; 100,000,000 ; 1,000,000 ; 7,000,000
   (e) 86,000,000 ; 34,000,000 ; 67,000,000 ; 68,000,000 ; 15,000,000

2 (a)

A	*B*	*C*	*D*	*E*	*Total*
567	901	631	276	440	2,815
980	345	342	471	890	3,028
5,123	12	789	4,590	78	10,592
729	500	4,900	26	1,789	7,944
678	14,789	470	134	2,300	18,371
8,077	16,547	7,132	5,497	5,497	42,750

(b)

	A	B	C	D	E	Total
	476	888	123	957	100	2,544
	347	540	321	890	580	2,678
	7,469	97	110	1,923	145	9,744
	345	913	7,800	71	12,309	21,438
	789	9,560	900	651	1,000	12,900
	9,426	11,998	9,254	4,492	14,134	49,304

(c)

	A	B	C	D	E	Total
	999	34	89	276	120	1,518
	679	934	503	846	456	3,418
	6,320	57	765	3,123	52	10,317
	789	10	1,700	7	2,690	5,196
	900	15,900	550	678	7,800	25,828
	9,687	16,935	3,607	4,930	11,118	46,277

3.
7,457	321	789	7,821	567	730
− 276	− 41	−645	− 74	−439	−399
7,181	280	144	7,747	128	331

4.
371	429	631	492	671
× 43	× 92	× 71	× 83	× 74
15,953	39,468	44,801	40,836	49,654

693	391	733	642	711
× 21	× 84	× 21	× 33	× 11
14,553	32,844	15,393	21,186	7,821

5. (a) 19
   (b) 3,691
   (c) 2,594
   (d) 3,821
   (e) 9,642
   (f) 9,326
   (g) 2,567
   (h) 9,791

6 (a) 18 × 7 + 3 = 129
   (b) 16 × 8 = 128
   (c) 17 × 24 − 11 = 397
   (d) 77 + 77 ÷ 11 = 84
   (e) 9 × (121 ÷ 11) = 9 × 11 = 99
   (f) 17 × 8 ÷ (8) = 17
   (g) (80 ÷ [10] + 4 + [18] × 6) ÷ 5 = 24

1.10 Progress questions

1 Round off the following figures:

   To the nearest ten:
   44 ; 93 ; 79 ; 66 ; 7

   To the nearest hundred:
   374 ; 216 ; 319 ; 874 ; 51

   To the nearest thousand:
   6,749 ; 39,217 ; 39,921 ; 64,500 ; 47,216

   To the nearest million:
   6,792,431 ; 7,421,891 ; 33,333,333

2 Add up the rows and columns, and cross-check your answers.

A	B	C	D	E	Total
624	327	641	392	888	
719	461	333	471	777	
326	1,321	421	829	555	
3,174	19	932	666	429	
729	327	6,121	31	18	

3 Subtract the following:

6,721	862	333	4,221	8,219	621
− 399	− 74	−212	− 34	− 374	− 37

4 Multiply the following:

679	831	929	617	821
× 31	× 69	× 73	× 21	× 94

5 Divide the following:
   (a) 73,188 ÷ 19
   (b) 15,648 ÷ 24
   (c) 24,732 ÷ 36
   (d) 57,288 ÷ 88

6 Calculate the following mixed options:
   (a) (9 + 3) × 6 + 1
   (b) (11 − 4) × (8 − 2)
   (c) 15 × (11 + 4) − (66 ÷ 22)
   (d) 48 + 48 ÷ (5 + 3)
   (e) 8 × (63 ÷ [13 − 6])
   (f) 18 × 4 ÷ (16 − 4)
   (g) (32 ÷ [7 + 1] + 12 +[4 × 2] × 8) ÷ 10

Chapter 2
Fractions

2.1 Introduction to fractions
2.2 Fractions in their simplest form
2.3 Addition and subtraction of fractions
2.4 Multiplication and division of fractions
2.5 Review questions
2.6 Progress questions

2.1 Introduction to fractions

A fraction expresses part of a whole number. An easy example of how a fraction is obtained is to think about dividing a pizza. If one pizza is to be shared amongst 3 children equally the pizza is divided into 3 equal parts, as in Figure 2.1. If each child receives 1 of these 3 parts that is one third of the pizza, which in turn can be expressed as $\frac{1}{3}$.

Pizza Slices

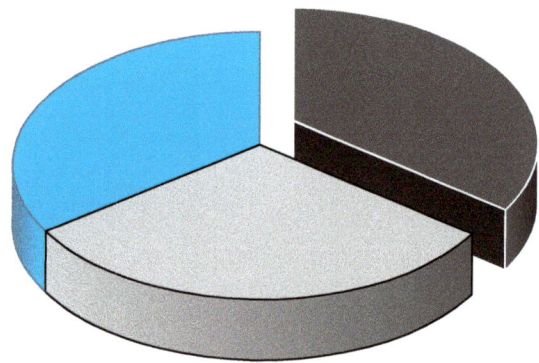

Figure 2.1 Pizza slices, pizza cut into 3 equal pieces

Example

If you were to split the profit from a business evenly amongst 6 shareholders they would each receive one of the six parts. This is one sixth of the whole, which can be expressed as $\frac{1}{6}$ and represented in Figure 2.2.

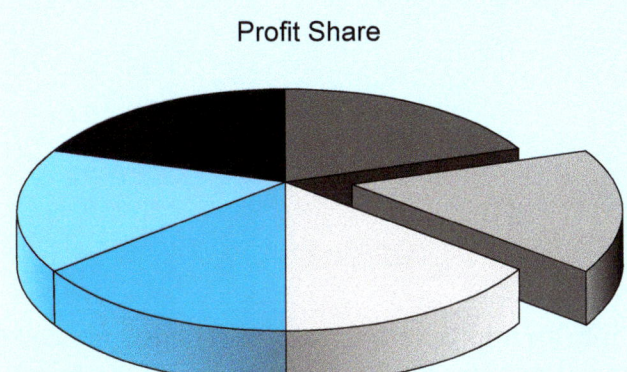

Figure 2.2 Profit allocation for shareholders

In a fraction the top number is called the numerator, and the bottom number is called the denominator. So, the 1 in the pizza example is the numerator whereas 3 is the denominator. In the profit example 1 is the numerator and 6 the denominator.

Where the numerator is smaller than the denominator (as in the examples above) the fraction is known as a proper fraction. This means that proper fractions will always have a value of less than one, that is they are parts of a whole number. Examples are $\frac{1}{3}, \frac{7}{8}, \frac{9}{10}, \frac{11}{12}$ etc.

The numerator however can also be greater than the denominator or equal to the denominator. This type of fraction is known as an improper fraction. An example of an improper fraction is as follows:

$\frac{63}{11}$

While a proper fraction is part of a whole, an improper fraction can also be written as a whole number and (usually) parts of a whole number which can be further expressed as a fraction; in other words, a mixed number (a mix of fractions and whole numbers).

So $\frac{63}{11}$ can be expressed a mixed number, that is a number containing whole numbers and fractions.

This is achieved by dividing 63 by 11, which produces 5 and a remainder of 8. In this case we would have a mixed number of:

$5\frac{8}{11}$

Example

Express $\frac{74}{9}$ as a mixed number.

As with the previous example, the numerator is divided by the denominator, that is 74 is divided by 9, which is 8 and a remainder of 2.

Therefore $\frac{74}{9} = 8\frac{2}{9}$

Example

$\frac{39}{4} = 9\frac{3}{4}$

It is also possible to change a mixed number into an improper fraction. To do this you need to multiply the whole number element of the mixed number by the denominator of the fraction part of the mixed number. Once this has been done the product of this calculation is added to the numerator part of the mixed number and the sum of this is then placed over the denominator.

Example

Expressing $6\frac{3}{4}$ as an improper fraction would involve the following steps:

(a) Multiply the whole number 6, by the denominator 4, which results in 24.

(b) Then add the numerator 3, to the result of step (a):

   3 + 24 = 27

(c) Finally place the sum over the denominator, which gives $\frac{27}{4}$

Except for intermediate calculations improper fractions are usually presented as mixed numbers.

Practice questions 1

Express the following improper fractions as mixed numbers:

(a) $\frac{13}{7}$

(b) $\frac{19}{6}$

(c) $\frac{29}{4}$

(d) $\frac{33}{8}$

(e) $\frac{47}{6}$

Practice questions 2

Express the following mixed numbers as improper fractions:

(a) $7\frac{1}{3}$

(b) $6\frac{4}{9}$

(c) $7\frac{3}{4}$

(d) $5\frac{2}{9}$

If the denominator and the numerator are the same, the fraction is a whole number.

Examples

$\frac{6}{6} = 1$ $\qquad$ $\frac{9}{9} = 1$

2.2 Fractions in their simplest form

When working with fractions it is good practice to express them in their lowest possible terms, that is their lowest possible numbers. Fractions can be reduced to lower terms if the numerator and denominator can be divided by the same integer to provide an integer. In other words, if the numbers can both be divided by a whole number we keep reducing the numbers until they can no longer be reduced any further to produce whole numbers.

Example

$\frac{6}{9}$ can be reduced further because both 6 and 9 can be divided by 3. So, by dividing both the numerator and the denominator by 3 the fraction reduces to $\frac{2}{3}$ which is its lowest possible term; it cannot be reduced further.

Example

$\frac{50}{100}$

Both numbers can be divided by 10, leading to an answer of $\frac{5}{10}$. However this is still not the lowest possible fraction because 5 and 10 can be divided by 5, giving an answer of $\frac{1}{2}$.

$\frac{50}{100} = \frac{5}{10} = \frac{1}{2}$

Both the numerator and the denominator must be divisible by the same number to reduce a fraction without any remainder. This reduction is known as cancelling down. The value of the fraction has not changed at all.

Practice questions 3

Express the following fractions in their lowest possible terms:

(a) $\frac{7}{21}$

(b) $\frac{34}{51}$

(c) $\frac{9}{72}$

(d) $\frac{10}{30}$

(e) $\frac{15}{75}$

(f) $\frac{9}{27}$

(g) $\frac{19}{95}$

In Section 2.3 we are going to add and subtract fractions. In order to do this we need to find a common denominator for the fractions. If we wish to add a fraction to another and they have different denominators we need to convert one, both, or all of the fraction(s) to have the same denominator as the other(s). So, if we wished to add $\frac{4}{12}$ to $\frac{3}{6}$ we would convert one of the fractions, so that it had the same denominator as the other. In this case I have chosen to convert $\frac{4}{12}$ into sixths.

To change the denominator (the twelfths in this case) to a required denominator (sixths in this case), divide the required denominator (6) by the existing denominator (12) and then multiply both the numerator and denominator of the fraction to be converted by this number.

Example

If $\frac{4}{12}$ is required to be shown in sixths, it would be done as follows:

Required denominator 6

Existing denominator 12

6 ÷ 12 = 0.5

Now multiply both the numerator and the denominator by 0.5:

$$\frac{4 \times 0.5}{12 \times 0.5} = \frac{2}{6}$$

The value of the fraction has remained the same, but it can now easily be added to $\frac{3}{6}$.

Practice questions 4

Convert the following fractions:

(a) $\frac{2}{6}$ to 12ths

(b) $\frac{2}{5}$ to 30ths

(c) $\frac{3}{9}$ to 27ths

(d) $\frac{7}{11}$ to 77ths

2.3 Addition and subtraction of fractions

When adding or subtracting fractions, it is imperative to have the same denominator, otherwise it is not possible to perform the calculation.

Examples

$$\frac{3}{8} + \frac{4}{8} = \frac{7}{8}$$

$$\frac{7}{9} - \frac{1}{9} = \frac{6}{9} = \frac{2}{3}$$

If the denominators are not the same, they need to be adjusted so they all have a common denominator (see Section 2.2 for more on this).

Example

$$\frac{2}{7} + \frac{3}{14}$$

In this calculation, the common denominator could be 14. This would be achieved by dividing 14 by 7. Because 7 goes into 14 exactly 2 times, the first fraction is multiplied by 2, producing:

$$\frac{4}{14} + \frac{3}{14}$$

The denominators are now both the same so the fractions can be added and the result converted to its lowest possible terms.

$$\frac{4}{14} + \frac{3}{14} = \frac{7}{14} = \frac{1}{2}$$

Where more fractions are added or subtracted, the calculation gets more complex because the three fractions must have the same common denominator. To keep calculations simple, we do not just use any common denominator, but we seek the lowest (value) common denominator (LCD).

Example

$$\frac{2}{4} + \frac{5}{8} + \frac{1}{3}$$

The LCD for these three fractions is 24 because all the denominators can divide into 24 exactly, but not into a lower number. An alternative to converting to 24 could be 48 because all the denominators would once again divide exactly into them. However, the calculations associated with the conversion are messier because the numbers are larger.

So, using 24 as the LCD the fractions become:

$\frac{2}{4} = \frac{12}{24}$ because 4 divides into 24 six times, so both the numerator and denominator are multiplied by 6.

$\frac{5}{8} = \frac{15}{24}$ because 8 divides into 24 three times, so both the numerator and denominator are multiplied by 3.

$\frac{1}{3} = \frac{8}{24}$ because 3 divides into 24 eight times, so both the numerator and denominator are multiplied by 8.

The calculation can now be performed as follows:

$$\frac{12}{24} + \frac{15}{24} + \frac{8}{24} = \frac{35}{24} = 1\frac{11}{24}$$

The result is a mixed number because 24 divides into 35 once, with 11 remaining. So we have a whole number, 1, and a fraction $\frac{11}{24}$, hence $1\frac{11}{24}$.

When mixed numbers as opposed to fractions are added together, the integers and fractions are dealt with separately. The sequence is as follows:

1 Add the integers together
2 Add the fractions together
3 Add the sum of the integers and fractions together.

Example

$$4 + 7\frac{1}{2} + 6\frac{3}{4} + 11\frac{1}{8}$$

$$= (4 + 7 + 6 + 11) + (\frac{1}{2} + \frac{3}{4} + \frac{1}{8})$$

$$= 28 + (\frac{4}{8} + \frac{6}{8} + \frac{1}{8})$$

$$= 28 + \frac{11}{8}$$

$$= 28 + 1\frac{3}{8}$$

$$= 29\frac{3}{8}$$

The principle for subtracting mixed numbers is much the same as adding them: integers first, then fractions.

Example

$6\frac{2}{3} - 1\frac{1}{6}$

$= (6 - 1) + (\frac{2}{3} - \frac{1}{6})$ integers first

$= 5 + (\frac{4}{6} - \frac{1}{6})$ subtract fractions using lowest common denominator

$= 5\frac{3}{6}$

$= 5\frac{1}{2}$ simplify

It is also possible to deduct fractions when the second fraction is larger than the first.

Example

$3\frac{1}{2} - \frac{3}{4}$ the mixed number needs to be converted to an improper fraction

$= \frac{7}{2} - \frac{3}{4}$

$= \frac{14}{4} - \frac{3}{4}$ then find the lowest common denominator and convert

$= \frac{11}{4}$

$= 2\frac{3}{4}$ then finally present as a mixed number

It is also possible to solve additions and subtractions where they appear together.

Example

$5\frac{1}{2} + 6\frac{2}{3} - 2\frac{1}{12}$

$= (5 + 6 - 2) + (\frac{1}{2} + \frac{2}{3} - \frac{1}{12})$ integers first, then fractions

$= 9 + (\frac{6}{12} + \frac{8}{12} - \frac{1}{12})$ find a lowest common denominator and convert the fractions

$= 9 + \frac{13}{12}$

$= 9 + 1\frac{1}{12}$

$= 10\frac{1}{12}$

Practice questions 5

(a) $\frac{1}{2} + \frac{1}{6}$

(b) $\frac{1}{3} + \frac{1}{9}$

(c) $\frac{1}{5} + \frac{7}{8}$

(d) $\frac{2}{6} + \frac{9}{12}$

(e) $\frac{3}{4} - \frac{1}{5}$

(f) $\frac{7}{8} - \frac{2}{12}$

(g) $\frac{5}{6} - \frac{4}{9}$

(h) $\frac{6}{7} - \frac{1}{3}$

(i) $2\frac{3}{4} + 4\frac{1}{2}$

(j) $6\frac{7}{8} + 7\frac{1}{16}$

(k) $7\frac{2}{5} - 4\frac{1}{10}$

(l) $4\frac{1}{2} + 6\frac{3}{4} - 2\frac{1}{8}$

(m) $7\frac{3}{8} + 7\frac{2}{6} - 1\frac{8}{9}$

2.4 Multiplication and division of fractions

There are two parts to this section. The first part deals with the multiplication and division of whole numbers and fractions, while the second part deals with the multiplication and division of fractions by fractions, as well as dealing with mixed numbers and fractions.

When multiplying a whole number by a fraction, the whole number is multiplied by the numerator and the product is placed over the existing denominator.

Examples

$\frac{3}{7} \times 8 = \frac{3 \times 8}{7} = \frac{24}{7} = 3\frac{3}{7}$

$\frac{4}{6} \times 17 = \frac{4 \times 17}{6} = \frac{68}{6} = 11\frac{2}{6} = 11\frac{1}{3}$

To divide a fraction by a whole number the denominator is multiplied by the whole number, and the existing numerator is placed over the product.

Examples

$$\frac{5}{6} \div 7 = \frac{5}{6 \times 7} = \frac{5}{42}$$

$$\frac{3}{4} \div 6 = \frac{3}{4 \times 6} = \frac{3}{24} = \frac{1}{8}$$

Practice questions 6

(a) $9 \times \frac{2}{5}$

(b) $18 \times \frac{1}{6}$

(c) $23 \times \frac{2}{9}$

(d) $\frac{11}{33} \div 7$

(e) $\frac{6}{11} \div 4$

(f) $\frac{17}{19} \div 6$

To multiply one fraction by another, the numerators are multiplied by each other and then the denominators are multiplied by each other, and the result is reduced to the lowest possible terms.

Examples

$$\frac{7}{8} \times \frac{4}{9} = \frac{7 \times 4}{8 \times 9} = \frac{28}{72} = \frac{14}{36} = \frac{7}{18}$$

$$\frac{6}{7} \times \frac{3}{9} = \frac{6 \times 3}{7 \times 9} = \frac{18}{63} = \frac{2}{7}$$

To divide a fraction by a fraction, the divisor is first turned upside down. The numerators of each fraction are multiplied by each other and the denominators of each fraction are multiplied by each other, and then expressed in their simplest form.

Examples

$$\frac{8}{9} \div \frac{4}{5} = \frac{8}{9} \times \frac{5}{4} = \frac{40}{36} = 1\frac{1}{9}$$

$$\frac{1}{4} \div \frac{1}{3} = \frac{1}{4} \times \frac{3}{1} = \frac{3}{4}$$

To simplify calculations, it is a good idea to reduce fractions to their lowest possible terms. Many calculations will have numerous fractions, and each should be reduced where possible, for example:

$$\frac{6}{12} + \frac{7}{14} + \frac{8}{72} + \frac{6}{36}$$

These can be reduced to:

$$\frac{1}{2} + \frac{1}{2} + \frac{1}{9} + \frac{1}{6}$$

$$= \frac{9}{18} + \frac{9}{18} + \frac{2}{18} + \frac{3}{18}$$

$$= \frac{23}{18}$$

$$= 1\frac{5}{18}$$

All of the procedures explained above apply to mixed numbers. However, in order to progress with the calculation, it is necessary to convert the mixed numbers into improper fractions.

Examples

$$6\frac{3}{4} \times \frac{1}{2} = \frac{27}{4} \times \frac{1}{2} = \frac{27}{8} = 3\frac{3}{8}$$

$$7\frac{7}{9} \div \frac{1}{4} = \frac{70}{9} \times \frac{4}{1} = \frac{280}{9} = 31\frac{1}{9}$$

Practice questions 7

(a) $\frac{3}{4} \times \frac{2}{3}$

(b) $\frac{3}{6} \times \frac{5}{7}$

(c) $\frac{4}{7} \times \frac{6}{9}$

(d) $\frac{6}{11} \times \frac{5}{7}$

Practice questions 8

(a) $4 \div \frac{3}{4}$

(b) $\frac{1}{8} \div \frac{1}{4}$

(c) $\frac{1}{7} \div \frac{1}{14}$

(d) $\frac{1}{6} \div \frac{1}{2}$

2.5 Review questions

1. Reduce the following fractions to their lowest possible terms:

   $\frac{7}{21}$; $\frac{13}{78}$; $\frac{38}{95}$; $\frac{75}{125}$; $\frac{54}{72}$; $\frac{21}{84}$

2. Convert the following fractions:

   $\frac{6}{9}$ to 54ths

   $\frac{7}{14}$ to 42ths

   $\frac{4}{16}$ to 64ths

   $\frac{3}{17}$ to 51ths

   $\frac{4}{18}$ to 36ths

3. Express the following mixed numbers as improper fractions:

   $7\frac{3}{9}$; $16\frac{4}{7}$; $13\frac{2}{4}$; $7\frac{6}{11}$; $8\frac{7}{9}$; $14\frac{2}{3}$

4. Carry out the following calculations:

   (a) $\frac{2}{6} + \frac{1}{12}$

   (b) $\frac{1}{9} + \frac{7}{18}$

   (c) $\frac{7}{14} + \frac{6}{56}$

   (d) $9\frac{1}{8} + 7\frac{2}{24}$

   (e) $11\frac{2}{4} + 12\frac{2}{12}$

   (f) $13\frac{1}{8} - 3\frac{2}{24}$

   (g) $8\frac{1}{7} + 19\frac{2}{14} - 6\frac{4}{14}$

   (h) $16\frac{2}{8} + 17\frac{1}{16} - 7\frac{1}{32}$

   (i) $15\frac{1}{8} + 17\frac{7}{16} - 6\frac{1}{4}$

5. Carry out the following calculations:

   (a) $15 \times \frac{3}{7}$

   (b) $35 \times \frac{1}{5}$

   (c) $23 \times \frac{6}{8}$

   (d) $19 \times \frac{7}{8}$

   (e) $\frac{3}{7} \times \frac{1}{4}$

   (f) $\frac{4}{9} \times \frac{3}{8}$

(g) $\frac{7}{9} \times \frac{8}{11}$

(h) $\frac{6}{11} \times \frac{17}{19}$

(i) $\frac{14}{21} \times \frac{3}{6}$

(j) $\frac{16}{19} \times \frac{17}{29}$

6 Carry out the following calculations:

(a) $6 \div \frac{2}{6}$

(b) $\frac{1}{3} \div \frac{1}{9}$

(c) $\frac{1}{7} \div \frac{2}{5}$

(d) $\frac{3}{8} \div \frac{2}{7}$

(e) $\frac{3}{18} \div \frac{7}{9}$

(f) $\frac{13}{18} \div 6$

(g) $\frac{19}{27} \div 7$

(h) $\frac{33}{41} \div 11$

Answers

1 $\frac{1}{3}$; $\frac{1}{6}$; $\frac{2}{5}$; $\frac{3}{5}$; $\frac{3}{4}$; $\frac{1}{4}$

2 $\frac{36}{54}$; $\frac{21}{42}$; $\frac{16}{64}$; $\frac{9}{51}$; $\frac{8}{36}$

3 $\frac{66}{9}$; $\frac{116}{7}$; $\frac{54}{4}$; $\frac{83}{11}$; $\frac{79}{9}$; $\frac{44}{3}$

4 (a) $\frac{2}{6} + \frac{1}{12} = \frac{4+1}{12} = \frac{5}{12}$

(b) $\frac{1}{9} + \frac{7}{18} = \frac{2+7}{18} = \frac{9}{18} = \frac{1}{2}$

(c) $\frac{7}{14} + \frac{6}{56} = \frac{28+6}{56} = \frac{34}{56} = \frac{17}{28}$

(d) $9\frac{1}{8} + 7\frac{2}{24} = 16 + \frac{3+2}{24} = 16\frac{5}{24}$

(e) $11\frac{2}{4} + 12\frac{2}{12} = 23 + \frac{6+2}{12} = 23\frac{8}{12} = 23\frac{2}{3}$

(f) $12\frac{1}{8} - 3\frac{2}{24} = 9 + \frac{3-2}{24} = 9\frac{1}{24}$

(g) $8\frac{1}{7} + 19\frac{2}{14} - 6\frac{4}{14} = 21 + \frac{2+2-4}{14} = 21$

(h) $16\frac{2}{8} + 17\frac{1}{16} - 7\frac{1}{32} = 26 + \frac{8+2-1}{32} = 26\frac{9}{32}$

(i) $15\frac{1}{8} + 17\frac{7}{16} - 6\frac{1}{4} = 26 + \frac{2+7-4}{16} = 26\frac{5}{16}$

5 (a) $15 \times \frac{3}{7} = \frac{45}{7} = 6\frac{3}{7}$

(b) $35 \times \frac{1}{5} = \frac{35}{5} = 7$

(c) $23 \times \frac{6}{8} = \frac{138}{8} = 17\frac{2}{8} = 17\frac{1}{4}$

(d) $19 \times \frac{7}{8} = \frac{133}{8} = 16\frac{5}{8}$

(e) $\frac{3}{7} \times \frac{1}{4} = \frac{3 \times 1}{7 \times 4} = \frac{3}{28}$

(f) $\frac{4}{9} \times \frac{3}{8} = \frac{4 \times 3}{9 \times 8} = \frac{12}{72} = \frac{1}{6}$

(g) $\frac{7}{9} \times \frac{8}{11} = \frac{56}{99}$

(h) $\frac{6}{11} \times \frac{17}{19} = \frac{6 \times 17}{11 \times 19} = \frac{102}{209}$

(i) $\frac{14}{21} \times \frac{3}{6} = \frac{14 \times 3}{21 \times 6} = \frac{42}{126} = \frac{1}{3}$

(j) $\frac{16}{19} \times \frac{17}{29} = \frac{16 \times 17}{19 \times 29} = \frac{272}{551}$

6 (a) $6 \div \frac{2}{6} = 6 \times \frac{6}{2} = \frac{36}{2} = 18$

(b) $\frac{1}{3} \div \frac{1}{9} = \frac{1}{3} \times \frac{9}{1} = \frac{9}{3} = 3$

(c) $\frac{1}{7} \div \frac{2}{5} = \frac{1}{7} \times \frac{5}{2} = \frac{5}{14}$

(d) $\frac{3}{8} \div \frac{2}{7} = \frac{3}{8} \times \frac{7}{2} = \frac{21}{16} = 1\frac{5}{16}$

(e) $\frac{3}{18} \div \frac{7}{9} = \frac{3}{18} \times \frac{9}{7} = \frac{27}{126}$

(f) $\frac{13}{18} \div 6 = \frac{13}{108}$

(g) $\frac{19}{27} \div 7 = \frac{19}{189}$

(h) $\frac{33}{41} \div 11 = \frac{33}{451} = \frac{3}{41}$

2.6 Progress questions

1 Reduce the following fractions to their lowest possible terms:

$\frac{6}{18}$; $\frac{19}{38}$; $\frac{34}{102}$; $\frac{18}{162}$; $\frac{15}{105}$; $\frac{57}{152}$

2 Convert the following fractions:

$\frac{3}{9}$ to 18ths

$\frac{7}{21}$ to 63rds

$\frac{8}{32}$ to 64ths

$\frac{9}{36}$ to 72nds

3. Express the following mixed numbers as improper fractions:

$6\frac{3}{4}$; $7\frac{9}{12}$; $21\frac{2}{6}$; $9\frac{2}{5}$; $8\frac{1}{3}$; $11\frac{1}{7}$

4. Carry out the following calculations:

   (a) $\frac{3}{4} + \frac{1}{6}$

   (b) $\frac{1}{7} + \frac{2}{5}$

   (c) $\frac{6}{13} + \frac{2}{26}$

   (d) $\frac{7}{49} + \frac{1}{7}$

   (e) $3\frac{1}{2} + 4\frac{1}{4}$

   (f) $6\frac{1}{9} + 7\frac{1}{3}$

   (g) $8\frac{2}{4} - 3\frac{1}{7}$

   (h) $9\frac{6}{11} - 7\frac{1}{6}$

   (i) $6\frac{1}{6} + 7\frac{2}{9} - 2\frac{1}{3}$

   (j) $13\frac{2}{7} + 14\frac{1}{6} - 3\frac{1}{7}$

   (k) $9\frac{1}{6} + 17\frac{1}{8} - 4\frac{1}{2}$

5. Carry out the following calculations:

   (a) $16 \times \frac{3}{8}$

   (b) $12 \times \frac{1}{4}$

   (c) $33 \times \frac{7}{11}$

   (d) $16 \times \frac{2}{12}$

   (e) $\frac{12}{17} \div 3$

   (f) $\frac{15}{29} \div 7$

   (g) $\frac{33}{55} \div 6$

Chapter 3
Decimals

3.1 Introduction to decimals
3.2 Rounding decimals
3.3 Converting fractions to decimals and decimals to fractions
3.4 Ratios
3.5 Percentages
3.6 Review questions
3.7 Progress questions

3.1 Introduction to decimals

A decimal is a number that contains a decimal point.

So, for example, 1.2 is a decimal and so is 0.3.

A decimal is often used as an alternative way to express a fraction. The numbers to the left of the decimal point represents whole numbers, while numbers to the right of the decimal point indicate part of a whole number and therefore a fraction of the whole.

Some more decimals:

(i)   0.10
(ii) 0.20
(iii) 0.50
(iv) 0.90

which can be represented by the following fractions:

(i)   0.10 = 10/100
(ii) 20/100
(iii) 50/100
(iv) 90/100

and can be expressed in their simpler forms as:

(i)   1/10
(ii) 2/10
(iii) 5/10
(iv) 9/10

or in their simplest forms:

1/10, 1/5, 1/2, 9/10

Here are some other decimals:

(i) 0.10
(ii) 0.01
(iii) 0.001
(iv) 0.0001

which can be represented by the following fractions:

(i) 0.10 = 1/10
(ii) 1/100
(iii) 1/1,000
(iv) 1/10,000

Hopefully you can see a pattern in these fractions: every place to the right of the decimal point represents division by an increasing factor of ten, as shown in Table 3.1.

Decimal point	First decimal place	Second decimal place	Third decimal place	Fourth decimal place
	Tenths 1/10	Hundredths 1/100	Thousandths 1/1,000	Ten thousandths 1/10,000

Table 3.1 Decimal places

Table 3.2 shows a set of six decimals and how they can each be represented by a fraction. (Note that each of the proper fractions has been given in its simplest form.)

Decimal	Tenths 1/10	Hundredths 1/100	Thousandths 1/1,000	Ten thousandths 1/10,000	As a fraction
0.1	1	0	0	0	1/10
0.30	3	0	0	0	3/10
0.125	1	2	5	0	125/1,000 = 1/8
0.50	5	0	0	0	5/10 = 1/2
0.0625	0	6	2	5	625/10,000 = 125/2,000 = 5/80 = 1/16

Table 3.2 Representing decimals as fractions

Practice questions 1

Put the following decimals into their simplest proper fractions:

(a) 0.70
(b) 0.850
(c) 0.810
(d) 0.4505

3.2 Rounding decimals

The rules for rounding decimals are like the rules for rounding whole numbers. If you were to round the number 13.**4**768 to the nearest tenth then you would be rounding the number 4 (the tenths value) up or down depending upon the number to its right. In this case, the number in the hundredths place to the right, 7, is greater than 5 so you would round up. So, the solution is 13.5. Note that all the numbers to the right of the rounded number are then ignored.

The example of rounding to the nearest tenth is the same as saying 'round to one decimal place' (see Table 3.1), while the task of rounding to two decimal places would be the same as rounding to the nearest hundredth.

To reinforce this concept, look at the examples in Table 3.3 where the decimals have been rounded to one decimal place and two decimal places.

Decimal	Tenths	Hundredths	Thousandths	Ten thousandths	Rounding to one decimal place	Rounding to two decimal places
0.173	1	7	3	0	0.2	0.17
0.3012	3	0	1	2	0.3	0.30
0.089	0	8	9	0	0.1	0.09
0.456	4	5	8	0	0.5	0.46
0.789	7	8	9	0	0.8	0.79

Table 3.3 Rounded decimals

Practice questions 2

Round the following decimals to 3 decimal places:

(a) 0.00896
(b) 0.00256
(c) 0.025689
(d) 0.7089

The important part in adding or subtracting decimals without the aid of a calculator is simply to ensure that numbers are aligned: that is, tenths are above tenths, hundredths align with hundredths and so on.

So, if you were to add up:

```
  15.2
   3.8    and
140.56
```

then to make calculations easier you would write:

```
  15.20
   3.80
 140.56
 ------
 159.56
```

Note that the only reason for placing zeros in this calculation is to make it easier to align.

3.3 Converting fractions to decimals and decimals to fractions

In Section 3.1 we saw how to represent decimals as fractions (see Table 3.2). We can also represent any fraction as a decimal by simply dividing the numerator by the denominator.

For instance, the fraction $\frac{1}{4}$ can be converted into a decimal by dividing 1 by 4 which provides the answer 0.25.

The improper fraction $1\frac{5}{6}$ can be expressed by ignoring the 1 and dividing the numerator of the fraction by the denominator, that is 5 divided by 6 which produces 0.83. Then add back the 1 to obtain the answer 1.83.

Practice questions 3

Convert the following fractions into decimals:
(a) 1/25
(b) 30/250
(c) 40/256
(d) 59/65
(e) 13/8

3.4 Ratios

A ratio is a comparison of two quantities by division. It shows the number of one quantity compared to another.

Ratios can be presented in two ways. A comparison of two quantities can be shown either as a fraction or using a colon. For more than two quantities we restrict the presentation to the use of colons.

Example

If there were 22 players in a football match and of these 3 were left-footed we could say that the ratio of left-footed football players to football players on the pitch would be represented by 3:22, which could also be represented by the fraction 3/22.

Example

A coin is tossed twenty times. On observation, it landed on heads five times and tails the remaining fifteen times. What is the ratio of heads to tails?

The answer would be 5:15 or 5/15, which of course could be further simplified to 1:3 or 1/3.

Example

A printing press produces 5,000 cards per second, of which 50 are currently failing in terms of the quality level set by managers. What is the ratio (expressed in its simplest form) of those failing to meet the quality standard in relation to the cards being produced?

At its first stage, the answer is 50:5,000 or 50/5,000, but of course this can be simplified to 1:100 or 1/100.

To compare three quantities, we would just use colons. So, for instance.

Example

A country's small army is made up of 1,000 soldiers. Of these soldiers, 500 are riflemen, 300 are artillery support soldiers and 200 are cavalry. This could be expressed as a ratio of 500:300:200, or in its simplest form 5:3:2.

To see how useful ratios of this nature can be look at the following example.

Example

The ratio identified in the previous example is the standard ratio for any army in that country. Using this ratio, identify how many riflemen, artillery support soldiers and cavalry there are likely to be in an army of 2,500?

The ratio in the previous answer was 5:3:2

To solve this problem, first sum the individual ratios together, so 5 + 3 + 2 = 10

To find the individual share for each category (in this case, type of soldier), divide the individual quantity ratio by the total of the individual ratios, then multiply this result by the total quantity you are trying to find the share of.

Formally, this is expressed as:

quantity ratio for a category divided by *total of the ratios* multiplied by *quantity*

So, in this case:

Riflemen = 5/10 × 2,500 = 1,250

Artillery = 3/10 × 2,500 = 750

Cavalry = 2/10 × 2,500 = 500

As a check, if you add up these individual categories they sum to 2,500.

Another example of using this type of ratio in a business scenario can be found below.

Example

Three students came together just over a year ago to start up a new business. Using various relatives as sources of finance they invested the following sums in their new business:

Student	Amount invested
Mo	£16,000
John	£9,000
Mustafa	£5,000

After the first year they earned a profit of £150,000. If the profits are to be shared on the basis of the amount invested, then the ratio of the relative amounts of money invested can be used to work out the share that each student will receive.

To do this, first sum the quantity ratios; that is, add the individual contributions together.

£16,000 + £9,000 + £5,000 = £30,000

Then, to work out the individual profit shares, use a similar formula to the previous example. Notice that the previous example used the calculated ratios: 5 riflemen/10 soldiers, etc. However, we could have used the number of riflemen in the original army of 1,000 soldiers (500 riflemen/1,000 soldiers) because the ratio is the same. This give us the formula that we will use:

quantity for a category divided by *total of all categories* multiplied by *quantity*

where the *quantity for a category* is the individual student's investment;
the *total* is the sum of the individual investments; and
the *quantity* element is the profit

Therefore, the formula for this task is

individual investment/total investment × profit

Student	Share of profit
Mo	£16,000/£30,000 × £150,000 = £80,000
John	£9,000/£30,000 × £150,000 = £45,000
Mustafa	£5,000/£30,000 × £150,000 = £25,000

As a check, the profit shares add up to £150,000.

Practice question 4

A large container ship has unfortunately collided with the sea wall of a large port in Asia. After inspecting the claim their insurance broker identifies that the damage is covered by three different insurance companies that they need to claim from. These are called Alpha, Beta and Omega. The total claim is $450,000. The claim should be split amongst the three insurance companies using the following ratio. 4:5:6 where 4 represents Alpha, 5 Beta and 6 Omega.

Using this information work out the claims for each of the three insurance companies.

3.5 Percentages

A percentage (or percent) is a special ratio that compares a number to a 100 and is represented by the symbol %.

As an example, 71/100 = 71%, which also can be expressed as a decimal, 0.71. In this case you should note that a decimal can be expressed as a percentage by simply moving the decimal point two places to the right. So, 0.8365 could be expressed as 83.65%.

Examples

(a) 30 students in 100 have tablets. Therefore 30/100 = 30%.

(b) 15 out of 30 investors in a start-up prefer dividends to revenue growth. Therefore 15/30 prefer dividends, which can be expressed as 0.5 or 50%.

(c) 30 cars in a street containing 120 cars are silver. Therefore 30/120 = 0.25 = 25%.

Practice questions 5

Calculate the percentages for the following:

(a) If 15 out of 25 containers in a factory are full, what percentage of the containers in the factory are full?
(b) 6 out of 11 South African batsmen in a cricket team are right-handed. What percentage of the team are left-handers (presuming none are ambidextrous)?
(c) 36 out of 40 students in a class can speak a second language. What percentage of the students can speak a second language?

Percentages are useful in business and quite important in our personal financial lives because profits, interest, wages and salaries, and the tax we pay are based on percentage calculations.

To work out the percentage of a number, you simply convert the percentage to a fraction or decimal and then multiply it by the number you are trying to find the percentage of.

So, 15% of 80 can be worked out by multiplying 0.15×80, which is equal to 12.

Practice questions 6

Work out the percentages for the following:

(a) 25% of 125
(b) 33% of 900
(c) 40% of 150
(d) 18% of 90

As well as calculating the percentage of a number, we may want to ask what percentage one number is of another. For instance, what percentage is 12 of 120? To work this out, you simply divide the number you wish to know the percentage of by the other number, or more simply in this case:

12/120 = 0.1

This is a decimal, that is, the proportion that 12 makes up of 120. This decimal of course can be easily converted to a percentage by moving the decimal point two places to the right, which is effectively the same as multiplying by 100.

Example

What percentage is £100 of £800?

£100/£800 × 100 = 12.5%

Practice questions 7

What percentage is 85 of the following numbers?

(a) 170
(b) 340
(c) 150
(d) 50

The profit on a product sold by a business can be worked out by simply subtracting the costs of the product from the price achieved for the product. So, if a car seller sells a car for £2,000 and it cost the seller £1,500 the profit is £500.

We can work out how much this profit is as a percentage of the selling price by working out what proportion of the selling price it is and multiplying by 100 to achieve a percentage.

Profit/Selling price × 100

£500/£2,000 × 100 = 25%

This figure is the profit margin, that is the percentage of profit that this business earns on its sales.

Practice questions 8

Work out the profit margins for the following businesses:

(a) A washing machine retailer buys a washing machine for £175 and sells it for £300.
ii) A soft drink company sells cans of the company's beverages at £0.20, and they cost £0.12 to produce.
iii) A book retailer sells a book at £10. It cost them £5.60 from the publisher.

Percentages are quite useful for pricing decisions that need to be undertaken in business.

> *Example*
>
> A small bookseller is selling one of his bestselling books at £18. Colleagues at a trade fair tell him that they are achieving a profit margin of 25% at this price. He explains to them that, given the cost he must pay to his distributor, he is only achieving 20%.
>
> Using this information calculate the current cost that he pays to the distributor and the cost he should be paying to achieve a 25% profit margin.
>
> *Current cost*
>
> Given that the profit margin is 20% over cost, this means that the current selling price is 120% of the cost. Therefore, to work out the cost we divide the selling price by 120 and then multiply by 100 to provide the cost.
>
> £18/120 = £0.15
>
> £0.15 × 100 = £15
>
> As a check, £15 plus 20% = £15 + (£15 × 0.20) = £15 + £3 = £18
>
> *Profit margin required*
>
> The profit margin required is 25%, therefore the cost should be such that the selling price is 125% of the cost.
>
> Therefore, cost needs to be £18/125 × 100 = £14.40
>
> As a check, £14.40 plus 25% = £14.40 + (14.40 × 0.25) = £14.40 + £3.60 = £18

Another very useful purpose of percentages is to apply decreases or increase to numbers. If we wish to increase a number by a percentage we can work out the new value in two ways.

- The first of these would be simply to calculate the increase and then add it to the original number.

- A second way of answering this problem is simply to add the percentage as a decimal to 1 and multiply it by the original value.

Example

Mustafa has been promised a 5% increase in annual salary at the end of the year. Currently his annual salary is £25,000. How much will he be earning at the end of the year?

Using the first method, the answer would be:

Original salary = £25,000

Increase = £25,000 × 0.05 = £1,250

New salary = £25,000 + £1,250 = £26,250

Using the second way, the calculation would be:

(1 + 0.05) × £25,000

= 1.05 × £25,000

= £26,250

This is therefore 105% of the original (a 5% increase on 100%).

We can also reduce a number by a percentage using two different methods.

In the first way, we simply work out the percentage of the number and subtract it from the original number.

A second way would be to subtract the percentage decrease (as a decimal) from 1 and multiply it by the original number.

Example

Calculate a 15% reduction in 90.

Using the first method, start by calculating 15% of 90

0.15 × 90 = 13.5

Then subtract this change from the original

90 − 13.5 = 76.5

Using the second way, subtract the percentage decrease from 1 and multiply it by the original number.

(1 − 0.15) × 90

= 0.85 × 90

= 76.5

Example

A company usually buys 100 pallets of paper a month from a variety of different stationers. One of these stationers has suggested to the company that if they purchase solely from them, they will provide an 8% discount on the current cost of £600 per pallet. Calculate how much this would be worth to the company a month.

Cost per pallet after discount:

£600 × (1 − 0.08) = £600 × 0.92 = £552

To find the cost of 100 pallets, multiply by 100:

100 × £552 = £552,000

Usual monthly cost = £600 × 100 = £600,000

Difference in monthly cost:

£600,000 − £552,000 = £48,000

Practice questions 9

(a) Increase 85 by 20%
(b) Increase 450 by 15%
(c) Increase 60 by 120%
(d) Decrease 400 by 30%
(e) Decrease 6,000 by 22%

Percentages can also be used to measure changes in numbers, that is they can express increases or decreases in percentage form.

To work out a percentage increase in a number, first work out the difference between the original number and the new number, and then calculate this change as a percentage of the original number.

Example

The price of a printer cartridge was £12.50 in 2016 and £14.50 in 2017. What was the percentage increase in price?

First calculate the difference between the new and original prices.

New price − Original price = £14.50 − £12.50 = £2.00

Second, work out what this difference is as a percentage of the original. This is the percentage increase.

Difference as a percentage of original = £2.00/£12.50 × 100 = 16%

For decreases we undertake the same calculation as for increases. The only difference is that the answer will be negative.

Example

The average price of a litre of milk at six supermarkets has fallen from £1.60 to £1.52 over a six-month period. What is the percentage fall in the price of milk?

First calculate the difference between the new and the original price.

New price − Original price = £1.52 − £1.60 = −£0.08

Second, work out what this difference is as a percentage of the original, and this is the percentage decrease.

Difference as a percentage of original = −£0.08/£1.60 × 100 = −5 %

3.6 Review questions

1. Put the following decimals into their simplest proper fractions:
   (a) 0.60
   (b) 0.970
   (c) 0.420
   (d) 0.6775

2. Round the following numbers to 3 decimal places:
   (a) 0.078492
   (b) 0.04532
   (c) 0.00671
   (d) 0.07926

3. Convert the following fractions into decimals (to 2 decimal places):
   (a) 3/25
   (b) 40/360
   (c) 60/280
   (d) 67/75
   (e) 23/8

4. Three friends decide to set up a computer games company. They have different amounts of capital to invest in their new business. Their investments are as follows:

Kieran	£45,000
Tom	£70,000
JD	£35,000

Tom is the brains behind the business and agrees with the others to share the profit in the ratio of the capital that each has invested in the business. The profit for the first year was £80,000. What share of the profit did each person get (to the nearest £)?

5 (a) Due to a partial power cut in a factory, only 20 out of 80 machines are working. What percentage of machines are not working?
   (b) A sixth form college has 820 female students and 410 male students. What percentage of students are male (to 2 decimal places)?
   (c) Croatia has a population of 4 million. Each country that qualifies for the football World Cup finals is allowed to have a squad of 23 players. Croatia gets to the tournament. What percentage of the population does the squad represent (to 5 decimal places)?

6 Work out the percentages for the following:
   (a) 40% of 600
   (b) 39% of 11,700
   (c) 27% of 150
   (d) 17.5% of 200

7 What percentage is 95 of the following numbers?
   (a) 380
   (b) 285
   (c) 237.5
   (d) 60

8 Work out the profit margins for the following businesses:
   (a) A second-hand car dealer buys a car for £6,300 and sells it for £7,000.
   (b) An antique dealer buys an antique chair for £480 and sells it for £720.

9 A discount store usually sells a set of pens for £2.99, having paid £1.50 to buy the set. However, on Friday it sells the set for £1.99. I buy the pens on Friday. What was the shop's profit margin on this set of pens on Friday?

10 (a) Increase 75 by 40%
   (b) Increase 320 by 25%
   (c) Increase 70 by 130%
   (d) Decrease 700 by 15%
   (e) Decrease 5,500 by 23%

Answers

1 (a) 3/5
   (b) 97/100
   (c) 21/50
   (d) 271/400

2. (a) 0.078
   (b) 0.045
   (c) 0.007
   (d) 0.079

3. (a) 0.12
   (b) 0.11
   (c) 0.21
   (d) 0.89
   (e) 2.88

4. Total capital invested £150,000

   The profit is shared in the same ratio as the capital invested so:

   Kieran receives 45,000/150,000 × £80,000 = £24,000
   Tom receives 70,000/150,000 × £80,000 = £37,333
   JD receives 35,000/150,000 × £80,000 = £18,667

5. (a) 60/80 = 75%
   (b) Total number of students = 1,230
       Percentage of male students 410/1,230 × 100 = 33.33%
   (c) Squad represents 23/4,000,000 × 100 = 0.000575% = 0.00058%

6. (a) 240
   (b) 4,563
   (c) 40.5
   (d) 35

7. (a) 25%
   (b) 33.33%
   (c) 40%
   (d) 158.33%

8. (a) 10%
   (b) 33.33%

9. 24.62%

10. (a) 105
    (b) 400
    (c) 91
    (d) 595
    (e) 4,235

3.7 Progress questions

1. Put the following decimals into their simplest proper fractions:
   (a) 0.65
   (b) 0.15
   (c) 0.90
   (d) 0.56

2. Round the following decimals to 3 decimal places:
   (a) 0.0056
   (b) 0.0063
   (c) 0.0222
   (d) 0.713

3. Convert the following fractions into decimals
   (a) 1/20
   (b) 3/2
   (c) 4/5
   (d) 5/6
   (e) 1/8

4. Three French companies have recently invested in a well-established supermarket chain in the UK. The first company invested £200 million, the second company invested £350 million and the third £650 million. After two years' trading the supermarket chain has decided to pay £200 million in dividends to these three companies. Using the information about their investments and your understanding of ratio analysis, identify how the dividends will be paid to the French companies if the dividends they receive are based upon the size of the investments they made.

5. Work out the percentages for the following:
   (a) 8% of 12
   (b) 45% of 90
   (c) 20% of 10
   (d) 1% of 90

6. What percentage is 25 of the following numbers?
   (a) 150
   (b) 115
   (c) 175
   (d) 35

7. Work out the profit margins for the following businesses:
   (a) A computer retailer buys keyboards at £16 and sells them for £28.
   (b) A brewery sells its beer at £1.20 per pint, which costs them £0.72 per pint to produce.

8. (a) Increase 35 by 22%
   (b) Increase 65 by 15%
   (c) Decrease 540 by 9%
   (d) Decrease 400 by 20%

9. Six pieces of organic corn-fed chicken cost £3.50 in 2015, whereas in 2017 they cost £5.25. Work out the percentage increase in the price.

Chapter 4

Test your knowledge

This chapter consolidates what you have previously learnt in class and self-study. You should spend an hour on Paper 1 attempting the questions, before checking your answers.

4.1 Paper 1

INSTRUCTIONS:

1. This paper comprises 8 questions. All questions should be attempted
2. Clear presentation and derivation of answers is required
3. The number of marks is indicated at the end of each question
4. This assessment has 33 marks available in total

QUESTION 1

A   A supermarket is displaying the sales price of some of its kitchen products. Round off the following prices to the nearest pound:

    (a) £39.49 _____

    (b) £16.51 _____

    (c) £23.50 _____

    (d) £27.33 _____

(2 marks)

B   Round off the following sales figures to the nearest million:

    (a) £8,363,949 _____

    (b) £3,521,727 _____

    (c) £17,499,999 _____

    (d) £ 837,230 _____

(2 marks)

(Total: 4 marks)

QUESTION 2

Work out the answers to the following sums:

(a) $4\frac{1}{8} + 2\frac{3}{4} + 1\frac{1}{2}$

(b) $7\frac{2}{3} - 2\frac{1}{6}$

(c) $5\frac{3}{4} + 7\frac{2}{3} - 6\frac{1}{2}$

(Total: 6 marks)

QUESTION 3

Express the following fractions as percentages (answers to two decimal places):

(a) $\frac{5}{8}$ _____

(b) $\frac{3}{7}$ _____

(c) $\frac{6}{15}$ _____

(d) $\frac{7}{11}$ _____

(Total: 2 marks)

QUESTION 4

Four businesses, A, B, C and D, have the following proportions of men and women in their total workforce. For each business, express the number of women as a percentage of the *total* workforce (to two decimal places).

	MEN		WOMEN
A	4	:	1
B	9	:	4
C	7	:	14
D	6	:	5

	A
	B
	C
	D

(Total: 2 marks)

QUESTION 5

Three business partners, Tom, Kieran and Joy, share profits in the ratio 3:2:1. The profit for the year is £690,000. What was the amount, in £s, of each partner's profit share?

Tom	
Kieran	
Joy	

(Total: 3 marks)

QUESTION 6

A trader buys a car for £2,600 and sells it at a profit of 20% above the cost price

(a) What was the sales price of the car? (3 marks)

(b) Express the profit as a percentage of the sales price. (3 marks)

(Total: 6 marks)

QUESTION 7

Work out the answers to the following sums:

(a) $(6 + 3) \times 8 + 2$

(b) $(9 + 4) \times (11 + 2)$

(c) $15 \times (5 + 5) - (18 \div 9)$

(d) $32 + 32 \div (2 \times 4)$

(Total: 4 marks)

QUESTION 8

Four business partners share their profit as follows:

Kieran	30%
Mark	25%
Kelly	35%
Jassie	10%

The current profit for the partnership is £60,000. However, it is agreed that each partner will invest 15% of their profit share into a new business venture. How much will each partner have left of their original profit after their new investment?

Kieran	
Mark	
Kelly	
Jassie	

(Total: 6 marks)

4.2 Paper 1 answers

QUESTION 1

A   A supermarket is displaying the sales price of some of its kitchen products. Round off the following prices to the nearest pound:

   (a)   £39.49   _____

   (b)   £16.51   _____

   (c)   £23.50   _____

   (d)   £27.33   _____

(2 marks)

B   Round off the following sales figures to the nearest million:

   (a)   £8,363,949   _____

   (b)   £3,521,727   _____

   (c)   £17,499,999   _____

   (d)   £ 837,230   _____

(2 marks)
(Total: 4 marks)

Answers

A   (a)   £39.00
    (b)   £17.00
    (c)   £24.00
    (d)   £27.00

B   (a)   £8,000,000
    (b)   £4,000,000
    (c)   £17,000,000
    (d)   £1,000,000

QUESTION 2

Work out the answers to the following sums:

(a) $4\frac{1}{8} + 2\frac{3}{4} + 1\frac{1}{2}$

(b) $7\frac{2}{3} - 2\frac{1}{6}$

(c) $5\frac{3}{4} + 7\frac{2}{3} - 6\frac{1}{2}$

(Total: 6 marks)

Answers

(a) $8\frac{3}{8}$

(b) $5\frac{1}{2}$

(c) $6\frac{11}{12}$

QUESTION 3

Express the following fractions as percentages (answers to two decimal places):

(a) $\frac{5}{8}$ _____

(b) $\frac{3}{7}$ _____

(c) $\frac{6}{15}$ _____

(d) $\frac{7}{11}$ _____

(Total: 2 marks)

Answers

(a) 62.50%

(b) 42.86%

(c) 40%

(d) 63.64%

QUESTION 4

Four businesses, A, B, C and D, have the following proportions of men and women in their total workforce. For each business, express the number of women as a percentage of the *total* workforce (to two decimal places).

	MEN		WOMEN
A	4	:	1
B	9	:	4
C	7	:	14
D	6	:	5

	A
	B
	C
	D

(Total: 2 marks)

Answers

A 20%

B 30.77%

C 66.67%

D 45.45%

58

QUESTION 5

Three business partners, Tom, Kieran and Joy, share profits in the ratio 3:2:1. The profit for the year is £690,000. What was the amount, in £s, of each partner's profit share?

Tom	
Kieran	
Joy	

(Total: 3 marks)

Answers

Tom   £345,000
Kieran £230,000
Joy   £115,000

QUESTION 6

A trader buys a car for £2,600 and sells it at a profit of 20% above the cost price

(a) What was the sales price of the car? (3 marks)
(b) Express the profit as a percentage of the sales price. (3 marks)

(Total: 6 marks)

Answers

(a) £3,120
(b) 16.67%

QUESTION 7

Work out the answers to the following sums:

(a) $(6 + 3) \times 8 + 2$
(b) $(9 + 4) \times (11 + 2)$
(c) $15 \times (5 + 5) - (18 \div 9)$
(d) $32 + 32 \div (2 \times 4)$

(Total: 4 marks)

Answers

(a) 74
(b) 169
(c) 148
(d) 36

QUESTION 8

Four business partners share their profit as follows:

Kieran	30%
Mark	25%
Kelly	35%
Jassie	10%

The current profit for the partnership is £60,000. However, it is agreed that each partner will invest 15% of their profit share into a new business venture. How much will each partner have left of their original profit after their new investment?

Kieran	
Mark	
Kelly	
Jassie	

(Total: 6 marks)

Answers

Kieran	£15,300
Mark	£12,750
Kelly	£17,850
Jassie	£5,100

4.3 Paper 2

QUESTION 1

A Round off the following prices to the nearest pound:
- (a) £43.19
- (b) £72.49
- (c) £88.50
- (d) £106.74

(2 marks)

B Round off the following sales figures to the nearest million:
- (a) £7,924,321
- (b) £6,499,999
- (c) £13,647,001
- (d) £947,325

(2 marks)

(Total: 4 marks)

QUESTION 2

Work out the answers to the following sums:

(a) $3\frac{2}{16} + 6\frac{6}{8} + 2\frac{9}{18}$

(b) $6\frac{4}{6} - 1\frac{2}{12}$

(c) $9\frac{6}{8} + 3\frac{2}{3} - 4\frac{1}{2}$

(Total: 6 marks)

QUESTION 3

Express the following fractions as percentages (answers to two decimal places):

(a) $\frac{7}{8}$ _____

(b) $\frac{12}{15}$ _____

(c) $\frac{4}{9}$ _____

(d) $\frac{3}{11}$ _____

(Total: 2 marks)

QUESTION 4

Four businesses, A, B, C and D, have the following proportions of snakes and rabbits in their pet shops. For each business, express the number of rabbits as a percentage of the *total number of animals* (to two decimal places).

	SNAKES		RABBITS
A	4	:	1
B	9	:	4
C	7	:	14
D	6	:	5

	A
	B
	C
	D

(Total: 2 marks)

QUESTION 5

Three business partners, A, B and C share profits in the ratio 4:5:1. The profit for the year is £300,000. What was the amount, in £s, of each partner's profit share?

A	
B	
C	

(Total: 3 marks)

QUESTION 6

A trader buys an item for £8,100 and sells it at a profit of 30% above the cost price.

(a) What was the sales price of the item? (3 marks)

(b) Express the profit as a percentage of the sales price. (3 marks)

(Total: 6 marks)

QUESTION 7

Work out the answers to the following sums:

(a) $(4 + 3) \times 5 + 4$

(b) $(6 + 3) \times (12 + 4)$

(c) $12 \times (7 + 7) - (16 \div 4)$

(d) $45 + 45 \div (9 \times 1)$

(Total: 4 marks)

QUESTION 8

Four business partners share their profit as follows:

Winnie	25%
Tigger	15%
Rabbit	40%
Eeyore	20%

The current profit for the partnership is £90,000. However, it is agreed that each partner will invest 10% of their profit share into a new business venture. How much will each partner have left of their original profit after their new investment?

Winnie	
Tigger	
Rabbit	
Eeyore	

(Total: 6 marks)

Chapter 5
Wages, salaries, taxes, depreciation, commission and discounts

5.1 Introduction
5.2 Wages and salaries
5.3 Taxes
5.4 Depreciation
5.5 Commission
5.6 Discounts
5.7 Review questions
5.8 Progress questions

5.1 Introduction

This chapter illustrates how the mathematical techniques and operations in the previous chapters can be used to solve business problems and facilitate people in undertaking the correct actions and decisions required in the 'real world'.

5.2 Wages and salaries

When most people are asked the question "What is your favourite day of the week or month?" they invariably say, "Pay day."

Weekly paid staff generally get paid on a Friday or a Saturday and their remuneration is known as wages, whereas monthly paid staff get paid on or around a specific date every month and their remuneration is known as a salary.

It may interest you to note that professional footballers, who can earn huge sums of money, are paid weekly by their club.

Examples

If a weekly paid member of staff gets paid £8 per hour and works a 35-hour week, they will earn:

£8 × 35 = £280 per week

before the deduction of taxation, national insurance and any other statutory deductions.

A monthly paid member of staff may earn £24,000 per annum, which means that their monthly salary is:

£24,000 ÷ 12 months = £2,000 per month

before any deductions.

It is custom and practice that weekly paid staff may be paid overtime if they work more than their contracted hours.

Example

Mary works a 40-hour week and earns £10 per hour. However, if she works any overtime beyond 40 hours she will earn 'time and a half' i.e. 1.5 times her hourly rate. This week she works 45 hours, so her wage is calculated as follows:

40 hours at £10 per hour	£400
5 hours at (1.5 × £10) = 5 hours at £15 per hour	£75
Total earnings for the week therefore	£475

On some occasions, particularly bank holidays or Christmas and New Year, employees may get paid double time, i.e. 2 times their hourly rate, so Mary could get £20 (2 × £10) per hour over Christmas.

Practice questions 1

1. Anne gets paid £15 per hour for working a 35-hour week. Any hours worked over and above that she gets paid time and a half per hour. In week 1 Anne works 38 hours in total, and in week 2 she works 41 hours in total.

    (a) What were her total earnings for the two weeks?
    (b) She is asked if she would like to work on Saturdays for 7 hours at double time (twice her normal rate). What does she now earn for the two weeks, including the Saturdays?

2. Bob, a builder, works 35 hours a week, and is paid £11 per hour. He works overtime for two weeks.

    In the first week, he works 8 hours at a time and a half rate of pay, plus two hours at double time.

    In the second week, he works an extra 10 hours at time and a half plus 6 hours at double time.

    How much did he earn in total over the two weeks?

3 Anita works a 40-hour week, getting paid £15 per hour.

   In week 1 she gets to work an extra 5 hours, 3 at time and a half and 2 at double time.

   In week 2 she works an extra 8 hours. 4 at time and a half and 4 at double time.

   What are her total earnings for the two weeks?

5.3 Taxes

There are three certainties in life: taxes, death and change.

Personal taxes are used for the benefit of society. If one can earn more than a certain tax free amount, then taxation is due on the amount earned above the allocated tax free level. The tax free level is known as a personal allowance. In the UK, the personal allowance in the 2017/18 tax year was £11,500. Any amount earned between £11,501 and £45,000 was taxed at 20%.

Example

Joe earns £39,000 per annum as a full-time employee chef. How much tax is he liable for?

Earnings	£39,000
Less his Personal allowance	£11,500
Taxable pay therefore	£27,500

Tax liability: 20% × £27,500 = £5,500

The total earnings of £39,000 are known as gross pay, i.e. pay before deductions. The net pay is the pay after deductions, which would be £39,000 − £5,500 = £33,500 in Joe's case.

In the UK, many employees have their tax deducted at source i.e. it is taken out of their weekly or monthly pay as a deduction. This system is known as PAYE (pay as you earn). The next time you get paid, check your pay/salary slip to examine the deduction.

Example

Dave earns £44,000 p.a. (per annum) and is entitled to his personal allowance of £11,500 p.a. Ignoring any other deductions, how much does Dave earn net per month? The tax rate is 20%.

Earnings	£44,000
Less Personal allowance	£11,500
Taxable pay	£32,500

Tax liability: 20% × £32,500 = £6,500

Total earnings after tax: £44,000 − £6,500 = £37,500

Monthly salary is £37,500 ÷ 12 = £3,125 per month

Practice question 2

Stephen earns £36,000 p.a. and is entitled to a personal allowance of £11,500 p.a. The tax rate is 25%. What is Stephen's net monthly salary?

There are a variety of other taxes apart from income tax.

Corporation tax is paid by companies on the profit that is declared by the company. Many statutory rules apply to corporations, depending on the size of the company and so on. The rate of corporation tax in the UK varies, being set at 18% for 2020/21, 19% p.a. for 2017/18–2019/20, and 20% p.a. in previous years.

Value added tax (VAT) is paid on most goods and services, although some are exempt, e.g. children's clothes. VAT is collected by businesses and paid to the tax authorities. The standard rate of VAT in the UK in 2019/20 is 20%.

Example

The prices of the items listed below are the selling prices of these items before VAT. Calculate the selling price of the items if 20% VAT needs to be added:

Item 1	£300
Item 2	£750
Item 3	£670
Item 4	£300

The calculation required is to find 20% of the price of the item before VAT, and then add that to the price before VAT to achieve the selling price plus VAT.

Therefore:

		VAT	Selling price including VAT
Item 1	£300	£60	£360
Item 2	£750	£150	£900
Item 3	£670	£134	£804
Item 4	£300	£60	£360

Practice questions 3

Calculate the selling price of the following items, if VAT at 25% needs to be added:

	Price
Item 1	£250
Item 2	£930
Item 3	£650
Item 4	£1,220

5.4 Depreciation

The idea that any fixed asset such as a car will maintain its value after it has been purchased or used is highly improbable. However, there are many exceptions, such as paintings, rare vehicles, properties in expensive areas like Mayfair in London and so on.

However, if you buy a new car, its value immediately reduces as you drive it away from the showroom. The more you drive it and the older it gets, the less valuable it becomes, i.e. it depreciates in value.

This depreciation of an asset applies to many other assets such as machinery or computers which are used in the manufacturing industry and elsewhere. The rate of depreciation will depend on the nature of the industry and the asset.

Example

If a new piece of equipment is bought for £100,000 and its life expectancy is 5 years, a manager may assume that the value of the asset depreciates evenly over its life. In other words, it depreciates in a straight-line way (so-called because if we plotted depreciation against time, we would obtain a straight line).

To calculate the depreciation, the initial value of the asset is divided by the number of years the asset is expected to last. So, in this example:

£100,000 ÷ 5 = £20,000 p.a.

Therefore, the asset depreciates in value by £20,000 p.a.

continued

Example continued

Depreciation in value by £20,000 p.a. could be illustrated as follows:

Year	Value after depreciation of £20,000 p.a.
Year 1	£80,000
Year 2	£60,000
Year 3	£40,000
Year 4	£20,000
Year 5	£0

Of course, not all assets are worth zero at the end of their lives. Many have a residual value, i.e. a resale value, so this part of the asset is not depreciated. If this is the case, subtract it from the asset's value before depreciation.

Practice question 4

A specialist instrument manufacturing company buys a precision cutting machine for £250,000. The machine has a useful life of 4 years and will be sold at the end of 4 years for £10,000. Calculate the depreciation each year if the company adopts a straight-line depreciation method.

5.5 Commission

Many companies employ sales staff and pay them a basic salary plus commission. The commission element of their pay represents a reward that is often a percentage of the sales that they make. The higher the sales, the greater the commission they earn. In some companies, the commission may be paid as a bonus, which is a fixed amount for exceeding a specified sales figure.

Example

Two companies are looking for sales staff.

Company X offers a basic annual salary of £80,000 plus a commission of 20% of the annual salary if a sales figure of £12 million is met.

Company Y is not offering an annual salary. It is offering a commission-only pay package, which is:

    0.6% on sales up to £6 million

    0.8% on sales between £6 million and £12 million

    1.00% on sales over £12 million

Assuming that the sales target of £12 million is met, which company gives the highest total pay?

Company X:

Annual salary = £80,000

Commission = $\frac{20}{100} \times \frac{80,000}{1}$ = £16,000

Total salary = £80,000 + £16,000 = £96,000

Company Y:

Commision of 0.6% on sales up to £6 million = $\frac{0.6}{100} \times \frac{6,000,000}{1}$ = £36,000

Commision of 0.8% on sales over £6 million = $\frac{0.8}{100} \times \frac{6,000,000}{1}$ = £48,000

Salary total = £36,000 + £48,000 = £84,000

Therefore, Company X pays better on sales of £12 million.

Practice question 5

Two companies are looking for sales staff.

Sigma Ltd offers an annual salary of £60,000 p.a. plus a guaranteed bonus of 15% of the annual salary, on condition that the target sales figure of £10 million is met.

Omega Ltd is not offering an annual salary. It is offering a commission-only pay package, which is:

0.5% on sales of insurance policies totalling up to £5 million, plus

0.75% on sales of policies totalling between £5 million and £10 million, plus

1.0% on sales above £10 million.

Assume the sales target of £10 million is met. Which company would give the highest total pay?

5.6 Discounts

Nearly everyone likes a bargain, and, given that sales are on at different times of the year, many 'bargain hunters' look for the best deal. Discounts are reductions offered on the 'normal' selling price. It is important to be able to calculate the discount offered so that you can compare prices.

Example

A washing machine is normally priced at £250. The store is offering a 10% discount. What is the selling price of the washing machine in the sale?

Normal price	£250
Less the discount (10% of £250)	£25
New selling price	£225

Practice questions 6

Calculate the following sales prices after the discount is offered on each item.

Item	Discount offered	Original price
A	10%	£600
B	18%	£200
C	12.5%	£800
D	16%	£90
E	33%	£300

5.7 Review questions

1. Steve gets paid £11 per hour and works a 32-hour week. He is paid time and a half for every hour worked over and above that, except on Sundays when he is paid double time per hour regardless of the number of hours worked during the week.

    Over two weeks, he worked the following hours:

    Week 1 – 38 hours during the week and 6 hours on Sunday

    Week 2 – 43 hours during the week and 7 hours on Sunday

    What did he earn in the 2 weeks, including Sundays?

2. Dave earns £38,000 p.a. and is entitled to a personal allowance of £11,850 p.a. The tax rate is 20%. What is Dave's net monthly salary?

3. Calculate the selling price of the following items which need to have a 20% rate of VAT applied to them:

    | Item 1 | £320 |
    | Item 2 | £690 |
    | Item 3 | £1,230 |
    | Item 4 | £180 |
    | Item 5 | £675 |

4. A car rental company buys 10 cars for £23,000 each. It retains the cars for five years and sells each car for £500 at the end of this period. The company uses a straight-line depreciation policy. Calculate the annual depreciation for all the cars for the period in question.

5 Two companies, Victoria Ltd and Angel Ltd, have advertised for sales staff. Victoria Ltd offers a salary of £35,000 p.a. plus a guaranteed bonus of 12.5% of the annual salary, on the condition that the annual sales target figure of £8,000,000 is met. Angel Ltd is not offering an annual salary. It is offering a commission-only pay package, which is:

0.4% on sales up to £6,000,000

0.7% on sales between £6,000,000 and £8,000,000

1% on sales over £8,000,000

Assume that the target of £8,000,000 is met. Which company would offer the highest total pay?

6 Calculate the discounted sales prices for the products below:

	Discount	Price (£)
Item A	15%	300
Item B	17.5%	350
Item C	30%	700
Item D	25%	600
Item E	10%	850

Answers

1 Steve's earnings (£)

Week 1	32 hours × £11 per hour		352.00
	6 hours × (£11 × 1.5)		99.00
	6 hours × (£11 × 2)		132.00
Week 2	32 hours × £11 per hour		352.00
	11 hours × (£11 × 1.5)		181.50
	7 hours × (£11 × 2)		154.00
Total earnings for two weeks			1,270.50

2 Earnings (£)   38,000
   Less personal allowance   −11,850
   Taxable pay   26,150

Tax liability = 20% × £26,150 = £5,230

Total earnings after tax = £38,000 − £5,230 = £32,770

Monthly salary = £32,770 ÷ 12 = £2,730.83 per month

3

		VAT @ 20%	Selling price (£)
Item 1	£320	64	384
Item 2	£690	138	828
Item 3	£1,230	246	1,476
Item 4	£180	36	216
Item 5	£675	135	810

4 Total cost of cars   10 × £23,000   230,000
   Less value after 5 years   10 × £500   − 5,000
   Total   225,000

   Depreciation each year £225,000 ÷ 5 = £45,000

5 Victoria's salary (£)
   Salary   35,000
   Bonus (12.5%)   4,375
                       39,375

   Angel's salary (£)
   0.4% on £6,000,000   24,000
   0.7% on £2,000,000   14,000
                        38,000

   Therefore, Victoria Ltd offers the highest total pay if sales are exactly £8,000,000.

6

	Discount	Price (£)	Discount (£)	Sales price (£)
Item A	15%	300	45	255
Item B	17.5%	350	61.25	288.75
Item C	30%	700	210	490
Item D	25%	600	150	450
Item E	10%	850	85	765

5.8 Progress questions

1. Diane is paid £11 per hour for working a 30-hour week. Any hours that are worked over and above the 30 hours in her working week are paid at time and a half per hour.

   (a) In week one, she works 27 hours, and in week two, she works 43 hours. What were her total earnings for the two weeks?

   (b) On the following Monday, which is a bank holiday, she is offered 8 hours work at double time (twice her normal hourly rate). She accepts the work. What are her total earnings for the two weeks and the additional Monday bank holiday?

2. Alan earns £39,000 per annum and is entitled to a personal allowance of £10,500. Ignoring all other deductions, how much does Alan earn per month, after he pays tax at 22% p.a?

3. Gary earns £800 per week, and works 52 weeks a year because he works abroad in Dragonland. His annual personal allowance is £11,600 per annum. The tax rate in Dragonland is 20% per annum. He gets paid at the end of the month and has worked for exactly one year. What was his monthly net pay?

4. Calculate the selling price of the following items after VAT of 22% has been added:
   (a) Inflatable boat (price excl. VAT £820)
   (b) Persian rug (price excl. VAT £740)
   (c) Fridge freezer (price excl. VAT £699)
   (d) Laptop (price excl. VAT £1,120)
   (e) Electric car (price excl. VAT £3,125)

5. A car leasing company buys 25 luxury cars at £50,000 each. The life of the cars is 5 years, after which each car will be sold for £5,000. Calculate the annual depreciation for the fleet of cars. The company adopts a straight-line depreciation policy.

6. Two companies – Polly and Peck – are looking for sales staff.

   Polly offers an annual salary of £65,000 plus a bonus of 15% of the annual salary if a sales figure of £13,000,000 is met.

   Peck does not offer an annual salary, as they pay on a commission only basis. The package that they offer is as follows:

   0.5% on sales up to £5,000,000; plus

   0.7% on sales above £5,000,000 up to £13,000,000; plus

   1.00% on all sales above £13,000,000

   If the sales target(s) of £13,000,000 are met, which company gives the greatest total pay?

7 Calculate the sale prices for the items in the table below after the discount is applied on each item:

Item	Original price	Discount offered
Mountain bike	£250	$7\frac{1}{2}\%$
Oven	£800	$12\frac{1}{2}\%$
Car	£25,500	17%
Blender	£99	10%
Jacuzzi bath	£12,500	20%
Hair clippers	£28	2%
Hoverboard	£333	$33\frac{1}{3}\%$

Chapter 6
Interest rate calculations and foreign exchange

- **6.1** Introduction
- **6.2** Simple interest and compound interest
- **6.3** Foreign exchange
- **6.4** Review questions
- **6.5** Progress questions

6.1 Introduction

There are two elements to this chapter. The first concerns the cost of money, i.e. interest, while the second concerns the price of one foreign currency in terms of another, i.e. exchange rates.

Many people need to borrow money at some point in their lives. It is very likely that they will have to pay interest to the lender for the money that has been borrowed. Banks and other lenders will advertise the rate of interest that borrowers need to pay for the loan, and this can vary from lender to lender because they are all trying to be competitive and win business. The rate of interest will also vary depending on the borrower's personal circumstances, the amount of the loan, the time period of the loan, and the collateral that may be available, as well as other factors.

The exchange rate is the price of one currency in terms of another. Exchange rates can vary quite considerably according to the economic performance of various countries. The rates we pay as individuals differ significantly from the prices that large companies and banks face.

6.2 Simple interest and compound interest

The two common categories of interest are known as simple interest and compound interest. While the calculations associated with these two methods of interest are similar, they can produce dramatically different results over multiple periods.

The following example shows how simple interest is calculated.

Example

If Sanja borrows £12,000 from the bank at 4% interest over 5 years, what amount of interest and capital will she have to pay back at the end of year 5 if she makes no repayments before the end of the loan?

The capital (or principal) is the amount of money that is being borrowed (the loan).

Principal	£12,000
Interest is 4% p.a.	£480 p.a.

The loan is for 5 years so the total interest to be repaid would be £480 × 5 = £2,400.

The total amount to be paid back at the end of year 5 is:

Principal	£12,000
Interest	£2,400
Total paid back	£14,400

Practice questions 1

(a) Elizabeth borrows £6,000 from her friend Paul, who has agreed to lend her the money for 3 years at an interest rate of 3.5% per annum (simple). How much will Elizabeth have to pay Paul at the end of year 3?

(b) Dave invests £10,000 in the bank for 5 years at a simple interest rate of 2%. How much interest has he earned in 5 years?

Compound interest is different from simple interest in that it is compounded each time period; that is, the interest earned in that period is added to the principal. Usually the time period is one year, and that is the period used in the examples below.

Interest is charged/earned on the total borrowed/invested (i.e. the principal plus interest earned in the previous time period), and not just on the principal as with simple interest.

In the case of a loan, the annual interest is added to the principal at the year end, and the interest charged for the following year is based upon the principal plus interest accrued from the previous year. To see how this works, look at the following example.

Example

If Andy borrows £4,000 from the building society for 3 years at 6% compound interest, how much would he need to pay the building society at the end of 3 years if he was to pay it all back in a lump sum?

Principal	£4,000.00	
Year 1 interest = 6% × £4,000	£240.00	
Amount owed at end of Year 1	£4,240.00	
Year 2 interest = 6% × £4,240	£254.40	added to the £4,240.00 accrued
Amount owed at end of Year 2	£4,494.40	
Year 3 interest 6% × £4,494.40	£269.66	added to the £4,494.40 accrued
Amount owed at end of Year 3	£4,764.06	

This is the amount to be repaid at the end of Year 3.

If this was a simple interest calculation at 6% p.a., then the interest payable would be:

Interest = 6% × £4,000 × 3	£720.00
Plus repayment of principal	£4,000.00
Total repayment	£4,720.00

From this example, you can see that when compound interest is charged, the total amount that is paid back to the lender is greater than when simple interest is applied to the loan. If you consider that our example used a relatively small amount of money, you can see that the type of interest chosen is very important for businesses that borrow or invest significantly larger amounts of money.

The same principles apply to investments, except that the saver will look for a higher interest rate and compound interest in order to achieve a better return.

Practice question 2

Richard lends his sister £15,000 as a deposit to buy a house in Liverpool. She promises to pay him back in 4 years. Richard charges his sister 4% p.a. compound interest over the 4-year period. How much, in total would Richard's sister have to pay him at the end of year 4 if she made no payments before the end of the loan?

It is also probable that when taking out a loan the period of time is not exactly one year. It could be for 1.5. 2.5 or 3.5 years and so on. It is also possible that interest may be payable every 6 months rather than on an annual basis.

Example

Lucas invests £50,000 for 18 months at compound interest of 5% p.a. which is paid into his account every 6 months. Calculate the total value of his investment after the 18 months has elapsed. Note that the interest rate is given as '% p.a.', in other words the annual rate of interest. Because interest is calculated for six months at a time we 'de-annualise' the rate using the following formula:

Interest rate = Annual rate × Months of interest compounding/12

So, the equivalent rate for 6 months at 5% p.a. becomes 5% × 6/12 = 2.5%

Investment		£50,000.00
6 months interest	2.5% × £50,000	£1,250.00
		£51,250.00
12 months interest	2.5% × £51,250	£1,281.25
		£52,531.25
18 months interest	2.5% × £52,531.25	£1,313.28
Investment		£53,844.53

Practice questions 3

Steve borrows £80,000 from his sister for 4 years at a simple interest rate of 6% per year. He lends the money to a friend, but at 8% compound interest per year for 4 years.

(a) How much does Steve repay, with interest, to his sister?

(b) How much does the friend repay, with interest, to Steve?

Practice questions 4

(a) If I place £30,000 in a bank at compound interest of 7% p.a., how much will be in the account at the end of 3 years?

(b) An alternative is to invest in a new business. It will give me the following income:
Year 1   £9,500   Year 2   £11,500   Year 3   £13,000
Would it be more profitable to invest my £30,000 in the bank or the business?

6.3 Foreign exchange

Holidays! Already everyone's interest has perked up. Most people only think about exchange rates when they are planning a holiday. Many countries have their own currencies, e.g. South Africa uses the Rand, so tourists need to plan their budgets in advance of the holiday. Many countries in Europe use the euro, whereas in the UK the currency is sterling. The exchange rate determines how much one currency is worth in relation to another.

Exchange rates

Foreign exchange bureaux use two different exchange rates: the selling rate and the buying rate. The difference between the two rates allows the bureau to make a profit.

For example, when I go to France the exchange rate for the pound to the euro is £1 = €1.12. If I exchange £1,000 for euros, I will receive:

£1,000 × 1.12 = €1,120

This is the selling price that I have accepted from the bureau.

When I return from France the buying rate is £1 = €1.20. If I come back with €1,120, I will receive:

€1,120 ÷ 1.20 = £933.33

Example

Bob goes to Germany for a week. He bought €2,000, paying in pounds. The exchange rate was €1.09 for £1. Bob returned at the end of the week with €300, and the bureau offered to buy back the money at €1.13 for £1. How much did Bob's trip to Germany cost him, in pounds?

Amount exchanged to take to Germany €2,000 ÷ 1.09 = £1,834.86

Amount brought back €300 ÷ 1.13 = £265.49

Total cost £1,834.86 − £265.49 = £1,569.37

The exchange rates between different currencies change constantly. A currency depreciates if there is a decrease in its rate of exchange against another currency. Depreciation is calculated as the change in the rate expressed as a percentage of the original rate.

Practice questions 5

A company is planning a project abroad and needs to buy euros. The exchange rate for euros in June 2018 was £1 = €1.31. In June 2019, the exchange rate was £1 = €1.16.

The company bought €300,000 in June 2018 and June 2019.

(a) What did it cost the company in 2018, in pounds?
(b) What did it cost the company in 2019, in pounds?
(c) By what percentage did the pound depreciate over the year?

Practice questions 6

Adam and his family were travelling around Europe. They used 300 litres of petrol which cost €1.38 per litre at an exchange rate of €1.17 to the pound.

(a) How much, in pounds, did the petrol cost them?
(b) What was the price per litre of petrol, in pence?

6.4 Review questions

1. Anita deposits £15,000 in a bank in Jersey for 5 years. The bank pays simple interest at 4% per annum. How much will Anita get back from the bank at the end of 5 years?

2. Diana borrows £40,000 from her Dad for 3 years at a simple interest rate of 3% per annum. She then lends the £40,000 to Robert at 2.5% compound interest for 3 years.
   (a) How much does Diana pay back her Dad at the end of 3 years (interest and capital)?
   (b) How much does Robert pay back Diana at the end of 3 years (interest and capital)?
   (c) How much profit or loss did Diana make?

3. Peter has £25,000 to invest. He can invest the total amount in a building society and get 4% p.a. at a compound interest rate for two-and-a-half years, or he can invest in a new business with a guaranteed return on his £25,000 of the following:

Year 1	£1,000
Year 2	£1,250
6 months	£600

   Which is the more profitable investment for Peter to make?

4. A foreign exchange dealer buys €500,000 in May 2018, when the exchange rate £1 = €1.11. In May 2019, the dealer buys another €500,000, when the exchange rate was £1 = €1.04.
   (a) What did it cost the dealer in May 2018, in pounds?
   (b) What did it cost the dealer in May 2019, in pounds?
   (c) By what percentage did the pound depreciate over the year?

Answers

1.
Principal deposited	15,000
Interest at 4% p.a. (£600 × 5)	3,000
Total return from bank	18,000

2. (a)
Loan	40,000
Interest at 3% p.a. (£1,200 × 3)	3,600
Repayment	43,600

   (b)
Loan to Robert	40,000
Year 1 interest at 2.5%	1,000
Repayment	41,000
Year 2 interest (2.5% × 41,000)	1,025
Amount owed at Year 2 end	42,025
Year 3 interest (2.5% × 42,025)	1,050.63
Amount owed at Year 3 end	43,075.63

   (c) Loss made by Diana £43,600 − £43,075.63 = £524.37

3 Principal   25,000
   Year 1   25,000 at 4%   1,000
   Total   26,000

   Year 2   26,000 at 4%   1,040
   Total   27,040

   6 months 27,040 at 2%   540.80
   Total   27,580.80

   Business investment   25,000
   Year 1   1,000
   Year 2   1,250
   6 months   600
   Total   27,850

   Therefore, the new business is the better investment for Peter to make (by £269.20).

4 (a) In May 2018
       €500,000 ÷ 1.11 = £450,450.45

   (b) In May 2019
       €500,000 ÷ 1.04 = £480,769.23

   (c) Depreciation
       1.11 − 1.04 = 0.07
       0.07/1.11 × 100 = 6.31%

6.5 Progress questions

1 Tammy deposits €20,000 in a building society for 6 years. She is paid 4% simple interest per annum. How much interest has she earned in the 6 years?

2 Peter borrows €1,500 from his sister for 3 years, paying her simple interest at the rate of 5% per annum. How much in total, including his loan would he have paid to his sister at the end of the 3 years?

3 Florence borrows €60,000 from her mum for 4 years at a simple interest rate of 3% per annum. She then lends the €60,000 to Tom for 4 years at 4% per annum, but at compound interest.
   (a) How much does Florence pay back to her mum at the end of the 4 years (interest and capital)?
   (b) How much does Tom pay back to Florence at the end of the 4 years (interest and capital)?
   (c) How much profit did Florence make?

4 John has €45,000 to invest. He has two alternatives. He can invest the total amount in a bank and get a compound interest of 6% per annum for 2 years, or he can invest in a new business venture, which will give him the following return on his €45,000 investment:

   Year 1   £6,000
   Year 2   £5,500

   Which is the more profitable investment for John to make?

5 Jas is planning to go to Cape Town on holiday.

   He will be in South Africa for two weeks, and exchanges £3,300 for South African Rand (R). The exchange rate is £1:R16.77.

   When Jas gets back from South Africa he has R10,580 left and decides to change it back into British sterling (£). The exchange rate on conversion is £1:R18.58

   How much in British sterling (£) did his expenditure on his two-week holiday cost?

Chapter 7

Test your knowledge

This chapter consolidates what you have previously learnt in class and self-study. You should spend an hour on Paper 3 attempting the questions, before checking your answers.

7.1 Paper 3

INSTRUCTIONS:

1. This paper comprises 7 questions. All questions should be attempted
2. Clear presentation and derivation of answers is required
3. The number of marks is indicated at the end of each question
4. This assessment has 33 marks available in total

QUESTION 1

(a) An item costs £220.00. VAT at 20% must be added to the cost. What is the selling price of the item including VAT?

(1 mark)

(b) You are paid an annual salary of £36,000 and your personal allowance is £4,800. If you pay income tax at a rate of 25%, what is your *monthly* salary after tax?

(3 marks)

(Total: 4 marks)

QUESTION 2

Carry out the following calculation:

(a) $5\frac{3}{4} + 7\frac{1}{8} + 3\frac{2}{9}$

(b) $9\frac{3}{8} - 7\frac{1}{4}$

(c) $8\frac{1}{9} + 4\frac{3}{7} - 3\frac{1}{3}$

(Total: 6 marks)

QUESTION 3

Work out the answers to the following sums:

(a) (7 + 6) × 9 + 4
(b) (8 + 3) × (7 + 4)
(c) 17 × (6 + 8) − (27 ÷ 3)
(d) 54 + 54 ÷ (3 × 6)

(Total: 4 marks)

QUESTION 4

Aaron, Shireen and Anita are business partners. They share the profit in proportion to the capital that they each contributed to the business. Their contributions were as follows:

Aaron   £37,500
Shireen   £50,000
Anita   £12,500

The profit for the business was £256,000 for the year ended 2018. What share of the profit did each partner get?

(Total: 3 marks)

QUESTION 5

(a) Two companies are looking for sales staff:

Sigma Ltd offers an annual salary of £70,000 p.a. *plus* a guaranteed bonus of 12% of the annual salary, on condition that the target sales figure of £10 million is met.

Omega Ltd is not offering an annual salary. It is offering a commission-only pay package, which is:

0.5% on sales of insurance policies totalling up to £4 million, plus
0.75% on sales of policies totalling between £4 million and £10 million, plus
1.0% on sales above £10 million.

Assume the sales target is met. Which company would give the highest total pay?

(3 marks)

(b) Pat works a 35-hour week and is paid a basic wage of £8.00 per hour. For two weeks she works overtime.

In the first week Pat works an extra 8 hours at time and a half, plus 4 hours at double time.
In the second week she works an extra 10 hours at time and a half, plus 6 hours at double time.

How much is the total pay that Pat receives for these two weeks?

(3 marks)

(Total: 6 marks)

QUESTION 6

The exchange rates of the euro against the pound were as follows (€s per £):

In September 2017   €1.26 equalled £1
In September 2018   €1.15 equalled £1

A UK company bought €200,000 in both September 2017 and September 2018.

(a) How much did the purchase cost *in £s* in 2017?   (2 marks)

(b) How much did it cost *in £s* in September 2018?   (2 marks)

(c) By what percentage did the pound depreciate over the year?   (2 marks)

(Total: 6 marks)

QUESTION 7

(a) If I put £28,000 into a savings account for 3 years with interest at a rate of 6% per annum compounded, how much will be in the account (in principal and interest) at the end of 3 years?

(2 marks)

(b) As an alternative I can make an investment of £28,000 in a new business, which will give me the following income:

     Year 1   £6,000
     Year 2   £9,300
     Year 3   £12,600

Which is more profitable for me: to leave the £28,000 in the savings account at 6% p.a. compound interest or to invest in the new business?

(2 marks)

(Total: 4 marks)

7.2 Paper 3 answers

QUESTION 1

(a) An item costs £220.00. VAT at 20% must be added to the cost. What is the selling price of the item including VAT?

(1 mark)

(b) You are paid an annual salary of £36,000 and your personal allowance is £4,800. If you pay income tax at a rate of 25%, what is your *monthly* salary after tax?

(3 marks)

(Total: 4 marks)

Answers

(a) £264

(b) £2,350 per month

QUESTION 2

Carry out the following calculation:

(a) $5\frac{3}{4} + 7\frac{1}{8} + 3\frac{2}{9}$

(b) $9\frac{3}{8} - 7\frac{1}{4}$

(c) $8\frac{1}{9} + 4\frac{3}{7} - 3\frac{1}{3}$ (Total: 6 marks)

Answers

(a) $16\frac{7}{72}$

(b) $2\frac{1}{8}$

(c) $9\frac{13}{63}$

QUESTION 3

Work out the answers to the following sums:

(a) $(7 + 6) \times 9 + 4$

(b) $(8 + 3) \times (7 + 4)$

(c) $17 \times (6 + 8) - (27 \div 3)$

(d) $54 + 54 \div (3 \times 6)$ (Total: 4 marks)

Answers

(a) 121

(b) 121

(c) 229

(d) 57

QUESTION 4

Aaron, Shireen and Anita are business partners. They share the profit in proportion to the capital that they each contributed to the business. Their contributions were as follows:

Aaron   £37,500
Shireen   £50,000
Anita   £12,500

The profit for the business was £256,000 for the year ended 2018. What share of the profit did each partner get?

(Total: 3 marks)

Answers

Aaron   £96,000
Shireen   £128,000
Anita   £32,000

QUESTION 5

(a) Two companies are looking for sales staff:

Sigma Ltd offers an annual salary of £70,000 p.a. *plus* a guaranteed bonus of 12% of the annual salary, on condition that the target sales figure of £10 million is met.

Omega Ltd is not offering an annual salary. It is offering a commission-only pay package, which is:

   0.5% on sales of insurance policies totalling up to £4 million, plus

   0.75% on sales of policies totalling between £4 million and £10 million, plus

   1.0% on sales above £10 million.

Assume the sales target is met. Which company would give the highest total pay?

(3 marks)

(b) Pat works a 35-hour week and is paid a basic wage of £8.00 per hour. For two weeks she works overtime.

In the first week Pat works an extra 8 hours at time and a half, plus 4 hours at double time.

In the second week she works an extra 10 hours at time and a half, plus 6 hours at double time.

How much is the total pay that Pat receives for these two weeks?

(3 marks)

(Total: 6 marks)

Answers

(a) Sigma   £78,400

   Omega   £65,000

   Therefore Sigma offer the higher pay.

(b) £936

QUESTION 6

The exchange rates of the euro against the pound were as follows (€s per £):

   In September 2017   €1.26 equalled £1
   In September 2018   €1.15 equalled £1

A UK company bought €200,000 in both September 2017 and September 2018.

(a) How much did the purchase cost *in £s* in 2017? (2 marks)

(b) How much did it cost *in £s* in September 2018? (2 marks)

(c) By what percentage did the pound depreciate over the year? (2 marks)

(Total: 6 marks)

Answers

(a) £158,730.16
(b) £173,913.04
(c) 8.73%

QUESTION 7

(a) If I put £28,000 into a savings account for 3 years with interest at a rate of 6% per annum compounded, how much will be in the account (in principal and interest) at the end of 3 years?

(2 marks)

(b) As an alternative I can make an investment of £28,000 in a new business, which will give me the following income:

Year 1   £6,000
Year 2   £9,300
Year 3   £12,600

Which is more profitable for me: to leave the £28,000 in the savings account at 6% p.a. compound interest or to invest in the new business?

(2 marks)

(Total: 4 marks)

Answers

(a) £33,348.45
(b) £55,900, so the business investment is more profitable.

7.3 Paper 4

QUESTION 1

(a) An item costs £530.00. VAT at 20% must be added to the cost. What is the selling price of the item including VAT?

(1 mark)

(b) You are paid an annual salary of £40,000 and your personal allowance is £8,000. If you pay income tax at a rate of 25%, what is your *monthly* salary after tax?

(3 marks)

(Total: 4 marks)

QUESTION 2

Carry out the following calculations:

(a) $6\frac{3}{4} + 8\frac{1}{8} + 4\frac{2}{9}$

(b) $9\frac{3}{8} - 6\frac{1}{4}$

(c) $8\frac{1}{9} + 5\frac{3}{7} - 3\frac{1}{3}$

(Total: 6 marks)

QUESTION 3

Work out the answers to the following sums:

(a) $(13 + 2) \times 6 + 4$
(b) $(7 + 2) \times (9 + 4)$
(c) $13 \times (3 + 7) - (18 \div 3)$
(d) $36 + 36 \div (2 \times 9)$

(Total: 4 marks)

QUESTION 4

Aaron, Shireen and Anita are business partners. They share the profit in proportion to the capital that they each contributed to the business. Their contributions were as follows:

Aaron   £43,000
Shireen   £28,000
Anita   £29,000

The profit for the business was £313,000 for the year ended 2018. What share of the profit did each partner get?

(Total: 3 marks)

QUESTION 5

(a) Two companies are looking for sales staff:

Sigma Ltd offers an annual salary of £60,000 p.a. *plus* a guaranteed bonus of 8% of the annual salary, on condition that the target sales figure of £10 million is met.

Omega Ltd is not offering an annual salary. It is offering a commission-only pay package, which is:

0.5% on sales of insurance policies totalling up to £4 million, plus
0.7% on sales of policies totalling between £4 million and £10 million, plus
1.0% on sales above £10 million.

Assume the sales target is met. Which company would give the highest total pay?

(3 marks)

(b) Pat works a 35-hour week and is paid a basic wage of £11.00 per hour. For two weeks she works overtime.

In the first week Pat works an extra 8 hours at time and a half, plus 4 hours at double time.

In the second week she works an extra 10 hours at time and a half, plus 6 hours at double time.

How much is the total pay that Pat receives for these two weeks?

(3 marks)

(Total: 6 marks)

QUESTION 6

The exchange rates of the euro against the pound were as follows (€s per £):

   In September 2017   €1.16 equalled £1

   In September 2018   €1.09 equalled £1

A UK company bought €250,000 in both September 2017 and September 2018.

(a) How much did the purchase cost *in £s* in 2017?   (2 marks)

(b) How much did it cost *in £s* in September 2018?   (2 marks)

(c) By what percentage did the pound depreciate over the year?   (2 marks)

(Total: 6 marks)

QUESTION 7

(a) If I put £35,000 into a savings account for 3 years with interest at a rate of 8% per annum compounded, how much will be in the account (in principal and interest) at the end of 3 years (to the nearest pound)?

(2 marks)

(b) As an alternative I can make an investment of £35,000 in a new business, which will give me the following income:

   Year 1   £6,000

   Year 2   £9,300

   Year 3   £12,600

Which is more profitable for me: to leave the £35,000 in the savings account at 6% p.a. compound interest or to invest in the new business?

(2 marks)

(Total: 4 marks)

Chapter 8
Tables, graphs and diagrams

8.1 Introduction
8.2 Tables
8.3 Graphs
8.4 Diagrams
8.5 Review questions
8.5 Progress questions

8.1 Introduction

This chapter deals with three quantitative tools, tables, graphs and diagrams. All three of these tools contain a common thread: they all provide ways for data to be presented and summarised in a clearer way than a narrative alone would provide.

8.2 Tables

You have already come across tables in Chapter 1 on arithmetic operations and, in particular, the operation of addition (Section 1.3).

Tables are used to represent data in an organised and a clear way. Table 8.1 (overleaf) is a simple table that shows the number of credit card transactions on different days of the week at a retail health food shop for the whole month of August 2019.

Tables are usually a two-dimensional presentation of data in a column and row format. Rows go across a table and columns go vertically up and down. If you look at Table 8.1, *Day of week* and *Number of transactions* are column headers while the actual days are row headings.

Day of week	Number of transactions
Monday	150
Tuesday	200
Wednesday	300
Thursday	258
Friday	400
Saturday	954
Sunday	562

Source: Neil's management accounts

Table 8.1 Credit card transactions at Neil's health food shop for the month of August 2019

Tables can be 'improved' by using totals or subtotals. So, Table 8.1 could be adjusted to show the total number of transactions, see Table 8.2.

Day of week	Number of transactions
Monday	150
Tuesday	200
Wednesday	300
Thursday	258
Friday	400
Saturday	954
Sunday	562
Total	2,824

Source: Neil's management accounts

Table 8.2 Credit card transactions at Neil's health food shop for the month of August 2019 with a total

Note that both of the tables include a source and a title, and that both variables (Day of the week and Number of transactions) are clearly labelled. This type of presentation for a table is known as 'good practice'.

In terms of how to design a table for a given data set, a general guide is that the design should be determined by the objectives of the table.

Such objectives could be:

(a) To present figures in a format that is easy to digest.

(b) To summarise a set of figures.

(c) To illustrate possible patterns in figures.

(d) To show relationships between figures (variables).

The following examples illustrate each of these objectives.

Example of presenting a set of figures

During August 2019 Neil's health shop had total sales of £7,500 on Mondays, £14,080 on Tuesdays, £18,868 on Wednesdays, £13,932 on Thursdays, £27,360 on Fridays, £80,820 on Saturdays, and £44,550 on Sundays.

Table 8.3 presents this data in a format that is easy to digest.

Day of week	Sales
Monday	£7,500
Tuesday	£14,080
Wednesday	£18,868
Thursday	£13,932
Friday	£27,360
Saturday	£80,820
Sunday	£44,550

Source: Neil's management accounts

Table 8.3 Daily sales totals at Neil's health food shop for the month of August 2019

Example of summarising a set of figures

If the shop owner wished to summarise the data in Table 8.3, a simple total would help. See Table 8.4.

Day of week	Sales
Monday	£7,500
Tuesday	£14,080
Wednesday	£18,868
Thursday	£13,932
Friday	£27,360
Saturday	£80,820
Sunday	£44,550
Total	£207,110

Source: Neil's management accounts

Table 8.4 Daily sales totals, with total, at Neil's health food shop for the month of August 2019

The total in Table 8.4 is the summation of all figures in the table, which is the total of the daily sales figures.

Practice question 1

A sales manager for a birthday card manufacturer wants to present his finance director with information on how sales of a new range of cards have performed over the last six months. The results were January 20,000 units, February 30,000 units, March 28,000 units, April 45,000 units, May 46,000 units and June 50,000 units.

Illustrate with a table how the sales manager could present the data.

Example of illustrating patterns in a set of figures

If the user of figures in Table 8.4 wished to see possible patterns in the numbers, they could use percentages and then present these in a tabular format.

So, for instance, Monday's sales as a percentage of total sales would be 7,500/207,110 × 100 = 3.62% and so on. The expanded information is shown in Table 8.5.

Day of week	Sales	Percentage of sales
Monday	£7,500	3.62%
Tuesday	£14,080	6.80%
Wednesday	£18,868	9.11%
Thursday	£13,932	6.73%
Friday	£27,360	13.21%
Saturday	£80,820	39.02%
Sunday	£44,550	21.51%
Total	£207,110	100.00%

Source: Neil's management accounts

Table 8.5 Daily sales totals, with total and percentage share of sales for each day in August 2019 at Neil's health food shop

The percentage figures in Table 8.5 show clearly how much each day of the week contributes to total sales. In this case, Monday is less than 4% while Saturday is nearly 40%.

Practice question 2

Use your answer to Practice question 1 to produce a table like Table 8.5. That is, add a 'Percentage of sales' column to the table you created to summarise card sales.

Example of showing the relationships between variables

If the shop owner wished to see possible relationships between different variables then data on another variable could be collected and posted into a new table alongside the previous figures. For instance, the sales in Table 8.4 could be compared to the number of credit card transactions. Assuming the data for credit card transactions has already been collected, then such a presentation could be presented as in Table 8.6.

Day of week	Sales	Number of credit card transactions
Monday	£7,500	150
Tuesday	£14,080	200
Wednesday	£18,868	300
Thursday	£13,932	258
Friday	£27,360	400
Saturday	£80,820	954
Sunday	£44,550	562
Total	£207,110	2,824

Source: Neil's management accounts

Table 8.6 Daily sales totals compared to number of credit card transactions each day in August 2019 at Neil's health food shop

Table 8.6 starts to illustrate the relationship. However, a better analysis would be provided by adding a percentage column for each variable along the lines undertaken in expanding the analysis shown in Table 8.4 to that in Table 8.5. The information in Table 8.6 would then be presented as in Table 8.7.

Day of week	Sales	Number of credit card transactions	Percentage of credit card transactions	Percentage of sales
Monday	£7,500	150	5.31%	3.62%
Tuesday	£14,080	200	7.08%	6.80%
Wednesday	£18,868	300	10.62%	9.11%
Thursday	£13,932	258	9.14%	6.73%
Friday	£27,360	400	14.16%	13.21%
Saturday	£80,820	954	33.78%	39.02%
Sunday	£44,550	562	19.90%	21.51%
Total	£207,110	2,824	100.00%	100.00%

Source: Neil's management accounts

Table 8.7 Daily sales totals compared to credit card transactions through percentages each day in August 2019 at Neil's health food shop

This analysis seems to suggest that there is a relatively strong relationship between credit card transactions and sales. In this case, a more useful analysis has been achieved by using percentages for comparative purposes.

Depending upon the objective of the user, the data could be presented in more than one presentation. For instance, Table 8.7 might be presented in a reduced format to show just the percentages, as in Table 8.8.

Day of week	Percentage of credit card transactions	Percentage of sales
Monday	5.31%	3.62%
Tuesday	7.08%	6.80%
Wednesday	10.62%	9.11%
Thursday	9.14%	6.73%
Friday	14.16%	13.21%
Saturday	33.78%	39.02%
Sunday	19.90%	21.51%
Total	100.00%	100.00%

Source: Neil's management accounts

Table 8.8 Daily sales totals and credit card transactions in percentage shares of totals each day in August 2019 at Neil's health food shop

Practice question 3

Using the data in Table 8.9 produce a table which identifies when sales of the new card range and sales of the old card range take place over the six-month period. (*Hint*: first, work out the percentage for each month of new cards relative to the total, then work out the percentage of old cards for each month relative to all sales.)

Comment on your analysis.

Month	Sales in units of new cards	Sales in units of old cards
January	20,000	31,500
February	30,000	30,000
March	28,000	29,900
April	45,000	22,500
May	46,000	19,600
June	50,000	17,000
Total sales	219,000	150,500

Source: Card company accounts

Table 8.9 Sales of new and old card ranges

Practice question 4

A large manufacturer of sterile bandages is considering reducing the number of products it offers for sale. After investigating two products that seem to be, to all intents and purposes, very similar – 'Vere' and 'Aldhere' – the directors are thinking about terminating one of the products in order to reduce distribution costs.

To facilitate such a possible decision one of the directors has collected information on the sales of the two products over the last two years. Table 8.10 shows the quarterly income from the two products.

Year	Quarter	Total sales	Vere Sales	Aldhere Sales
		£000	£000	£000
2017	1	4,500	3,200	1,300
	2	4,600	3,180	1,420
	3	4,700	3,020	1,680
	4	4,750	3,000	1,750
2018	1	4,800	2,900	1,900
	2	4,850	2,950	1,900
	3	4,875	2,975	1,925
	4	4,900	2,950	1,950

Table 8.10 Quarterly sales of Vere and Aldhere

Using the data in Table 8.10 construct a table that would allow a user to identify the performance of the two products in relation to total sales, and comment on your findings. (*Hints*: first, calculate total sales for each product, then Vere's sales as a percentage of total sales for each quarter, and then calculate Aldhere's sales as a percentage of total sales for each quarter. Calculate the percentage to one decimal place.)

8.3 Graphs

Table 8.11 shows the cumulative sales per hour of a large British-based book retailer for a 12-hour period on 12 October 2018. Note that the total is a cumulative total, which means that as we progress down the column each total comprises all of the sales that went before plus the current sales in that hour. For example, in Table 8.11 the total in the second hour interval is 196,000. This figure is made up of 108,000 for the first hour followed by whatever was sold in the second hour, that is 196,000 − 108,000 = 88,000. For the third hour the figure of 254,000 is made up of the previous 196,000 plus whatever was sold in the third hour: 254,000 − 196,000 = 58,000 units.

Time in one-hour intervals	Total sales of books (units)
1	108,000
2	196,000
3	254,000
4	299,000
5	362,000
6	435,000
7	490,000
8	525,300
9	557,300
10	602,300
11	655,300
12	701,300

Source: Company records

Table 8.11 Cumulative sales of books per hour on 12 October 2018

The graph in Figure 8.1 represents the data in Table 8.11, and is called a line graph. It is therefore an alternative way of representing the data in Table 8.11.

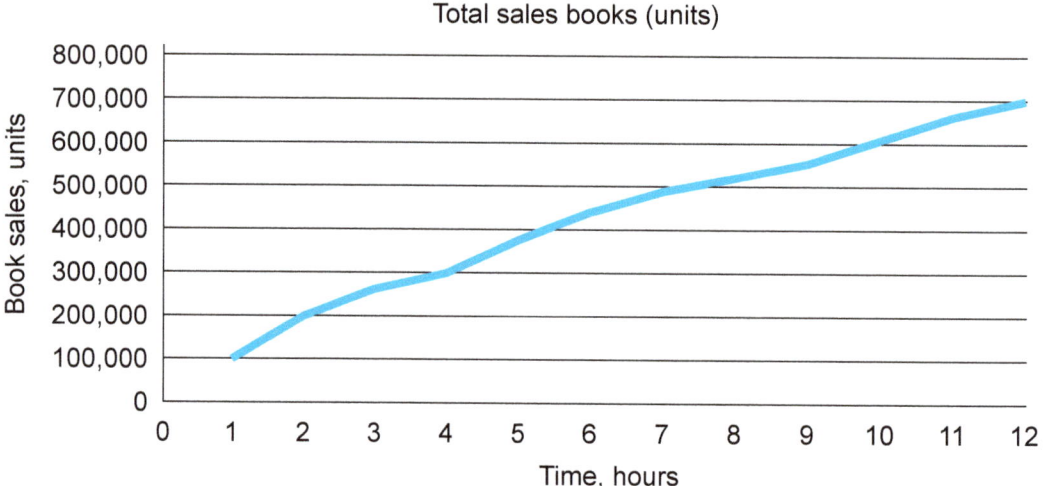

Source: Company records

Figure 8.1 Line graph of the sales of books per hour for a 12-hour period for a large British-based book retailer on 12 October 2018

Figure 8.1 is a line graph, it portrays the data in Table 8.11 using a continuous curve on a calibrated (or measured) scale.

The graph has two axes which are calibrated to reflect the variable they represent. In Figure 8.1 the vertical axis represents sales of books in units, while the horizontal axis shows the 12-hour period.

Both axes start from the same point, this point is known as the origin. At this point the value of both variables is 0. A movement along either axis, horizontal or vertical, represents a change in the variable it represents. These axes are both continuous in that an incremental movement along the axis and away from the origin represents an increase in the variable. Conversely, an incremental movement towards the origin indicates a reduction.

'Good practice' for charts is similar to that for tables. They should have a source and a title, and the axes (i.e. the variables) should be clearly labelled. The units of the variables should also be identified, so in Figure 8.1 the book sales are in units and the time is in hours.

Line graphs can also be used for comparing one variable against another. The variables must be given in the same units, so that may require conversion of the original data. Using our example of Neil's health food shop, we can compare the sales and credit card transactions shown in Table 8.8 because they have both been converted to percentages, as in Figure 8.2.

Graphs, however, are more powerful than just representing data. They can also be used for further statistical analysis, much of which is beyond the scope of this book.

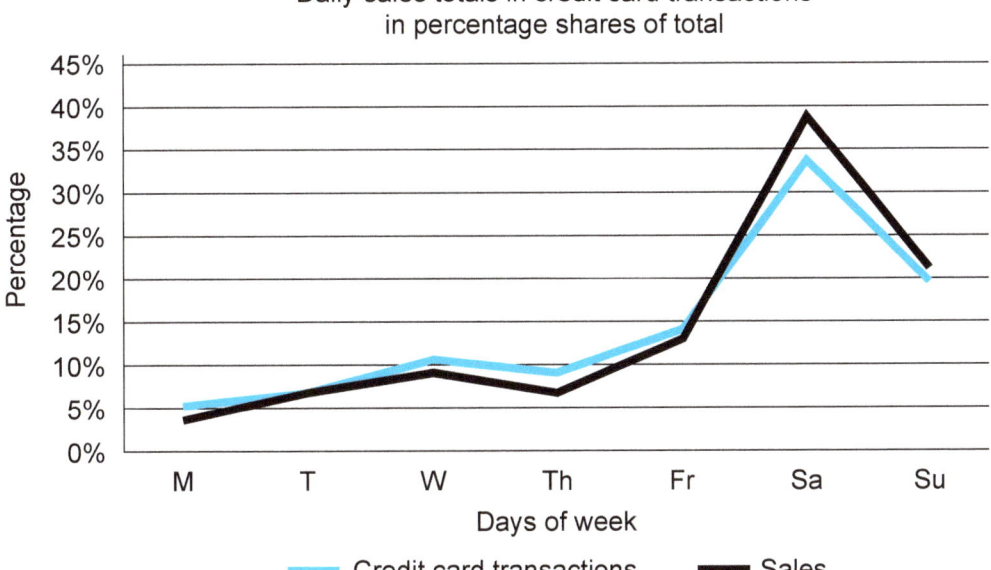

Source: Neil's management accounts

Figure 8.2 Line graph comparing sales and credit card transactions

8.4 Diagrams

An alternative visual representation of data is a diagram, sometimes called a chart. The difference between a graph and a chart is that the latter is more likely to be used when only one variable is represented.

An example of such a diagram is a bar chart as illustrated by Figure 8.3, which is based on the figures in Table 8.1.

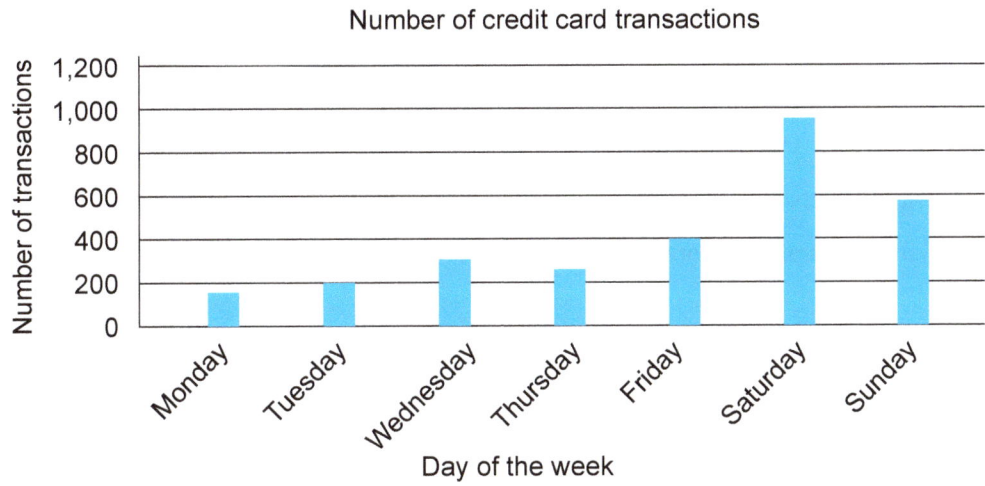

Source: Neil's management accounts

Figure 8.3 Simple bar chart

A bar chart can have horizontal rather than vertical bars, as in Figure 8.4.

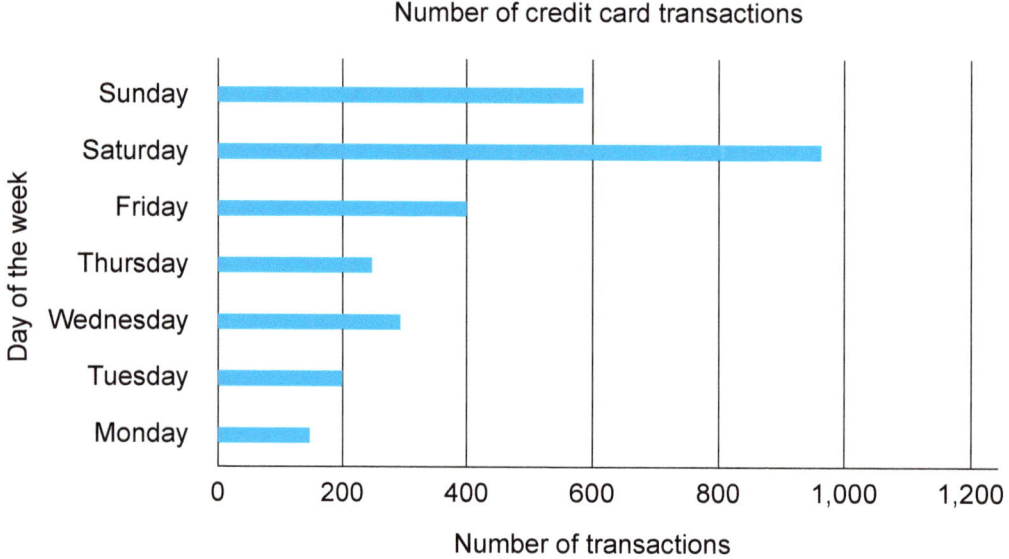

Source: Neil's management accounts

Figure 8.4 Horizontal simple bar chart

Alternatively, it could be three dimensional as in Figure 8.5.

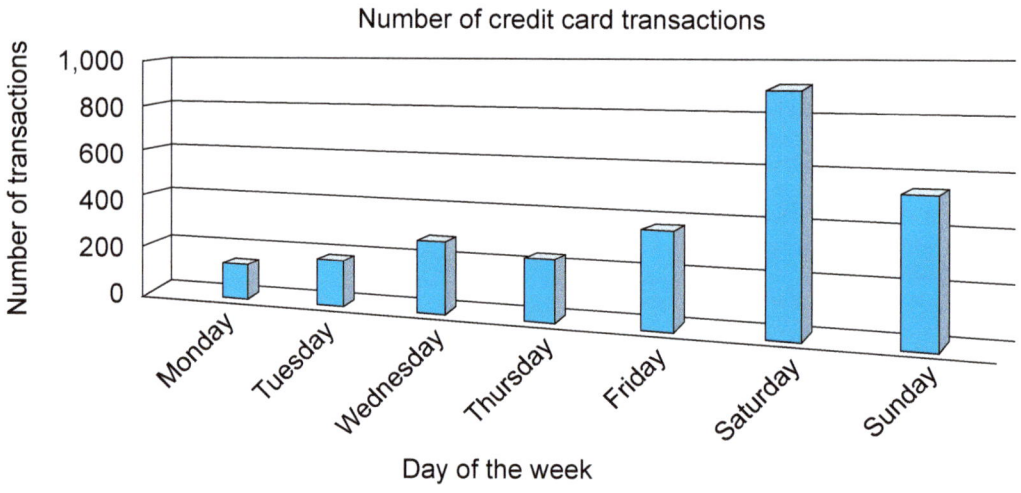

Source: Neil's management accounts

Figure 8.5 Vertical three dimensional bar chart

Simple bar charts are not the only way of representing data. The data shown in Figures 8.3 to 8.5 could be placed into alternative presentations, one example of which is the 'funnel' in Figure 8.6.

Source: Neil's management accounts

Figure 8.6 Funnel bar chart

Another way of representing data graphically is a pie chart such as that in Figure 8.7.

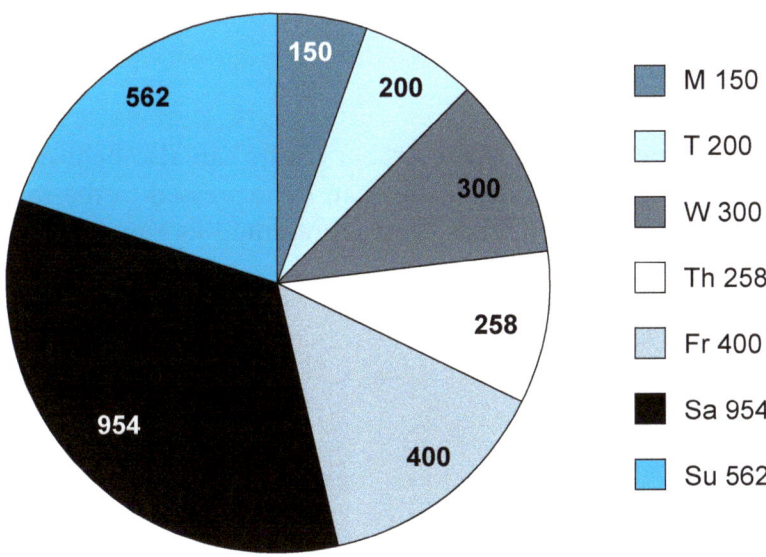

Source: Neil's management accounts

Figure 8.7 Pie chart

The advantage of a pie chart is that it allows the user to understand the importance of a segment to the whole. In Figure 8.7 the shop owner can see the significance of a day's credit card transactions in comparison to the total. For instance, how important Friday is to the whole.

To highlight the importance of a particular segment we could use an 'exploding' pie chart such as Figure 8.8.

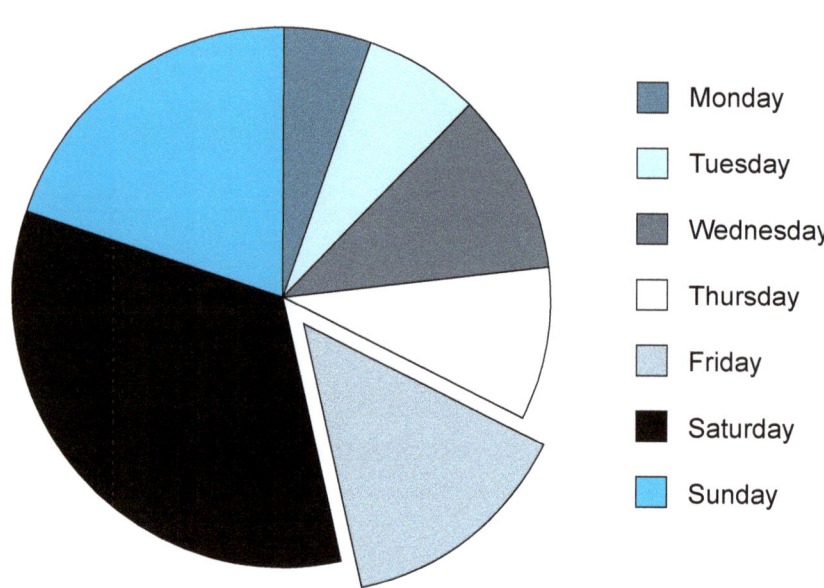

Source: Neil's management accounts

Figure 8.8 Exploding pie chart

The charts in Figures 8.3 to 8.8 contain one variable. However, bar charts can also be used to compare more than one set of variables with each other if they can be expressed in the same units. To illustrate this the information from Table 8.9 has been represented in a multiple bar chart, Figure 8.9.

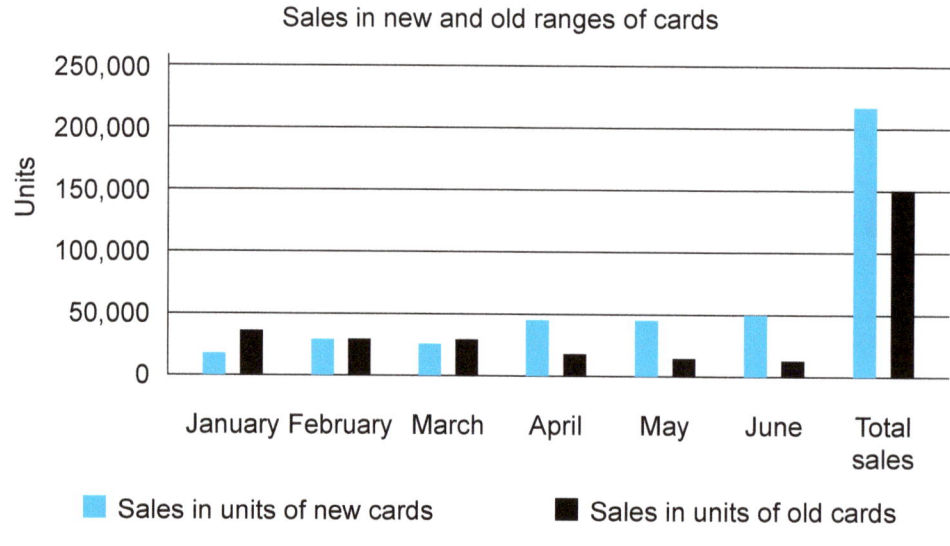

Source: Card company accounts

Figure 8.9 Multiple bar chart of card sales

Another example of this type of presentation is the representation of Table 8.8 in Figure 8.10, which allows a visual comparison of credit card transactions and sales at Neil's health food shop.

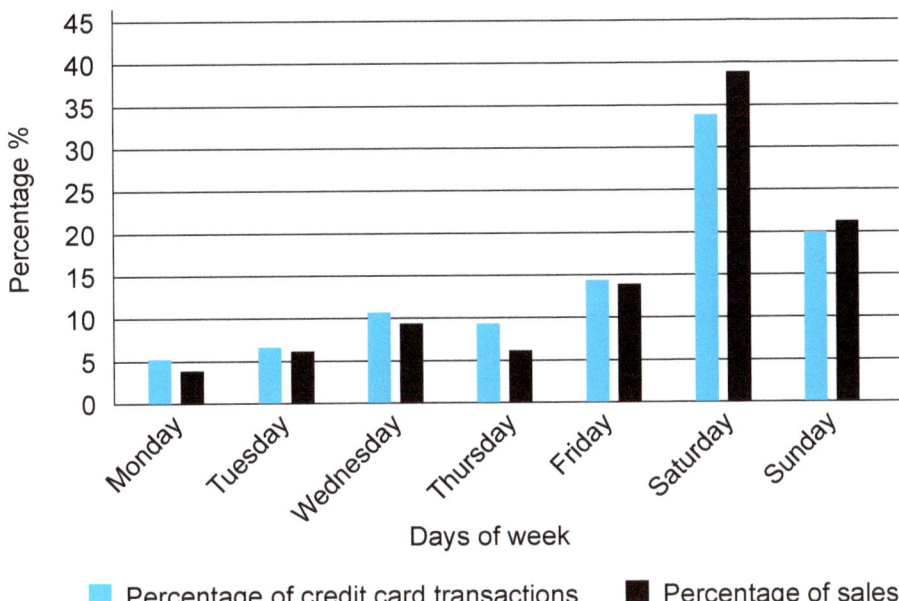

Source: Neil's management accounts

Figure 8.10 Comparative bar chart showing daily sales totals at Neil's health food shop for the month of August 2019

The information in Figure 8.10 can be presented in a variety of different presentations, as in Figures 8.11 and 8.12.

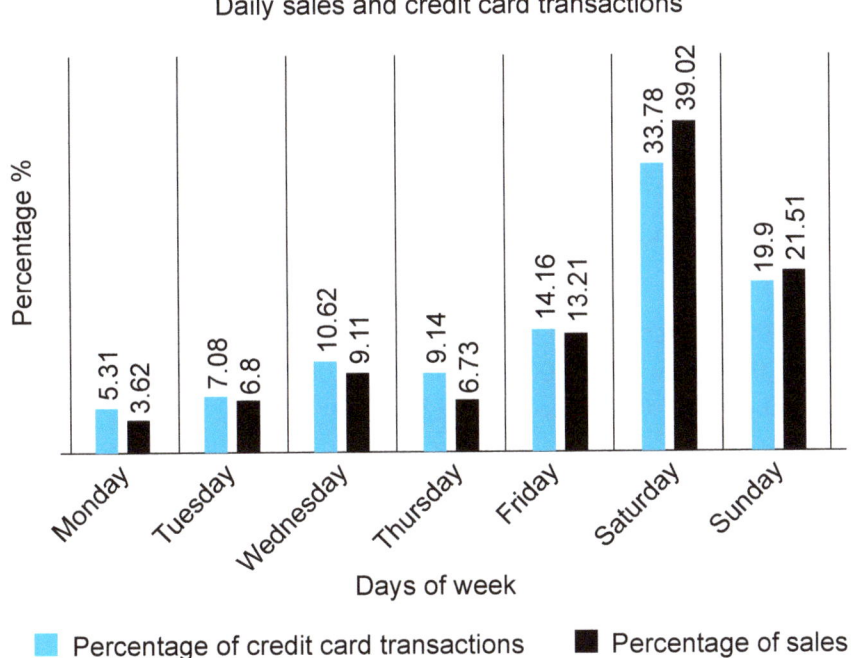

Source: Neil's management accounts

Figure 8.11 Comparative bar chart showing daily sales totals at Neil's health food shop for the month of August 2019 – alternative presentation 1

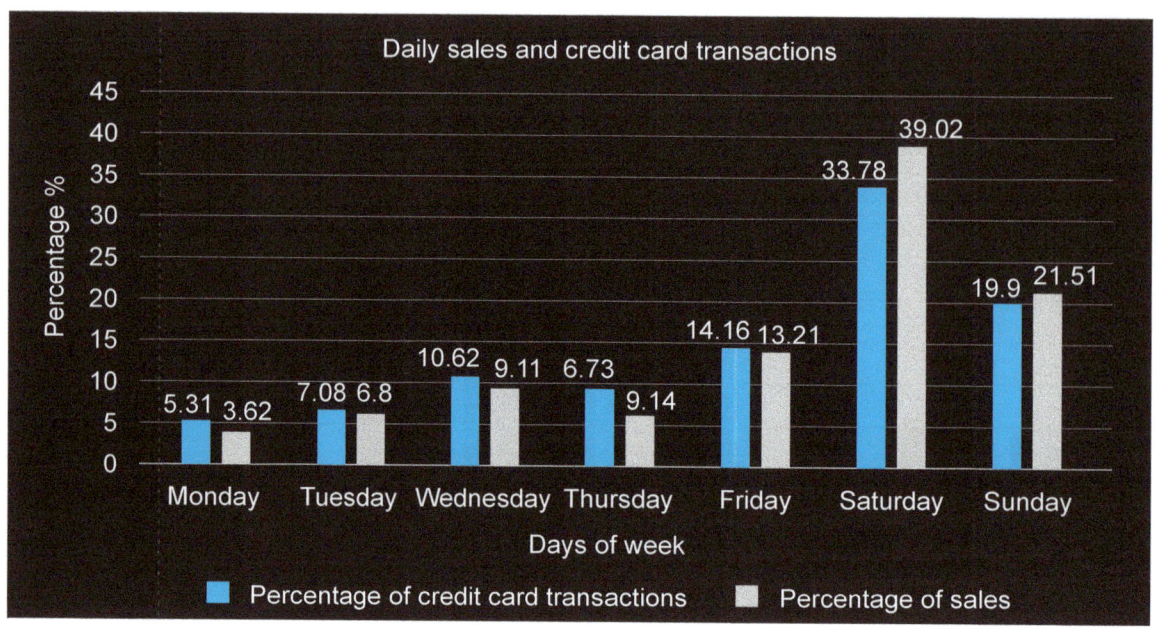

Source: Neil's management accounts

Figure 8.12 Comparative bar chart for daily sales totals at Neil's health food shop for the month of August 2019 – alternative presentation 2

Practice question 5

Produce suitable diagrams to illustrate the data in Practice questions 1, 3 and 4.

8.5 Review questions

1. The Cleary car body workshop is a medium-sized garage specialising in the repair of commercial vehicles. The Managing Director wishes to know how well sales are progressing in the year to December 2018.

    After spending several days collecting relevant information John in Finance has come up with the following data:

    Sales in January were £380,000, February £400,000, March £280,000, April £320,000, May £300,000, June £320,000, July £330,000, August £200,000, September £300,000, October £340,000, November £380,000, December £300,000.

    Using this data construct a table that could be presented to the Managing Director to illustrate sales progress.

2. Use the data below to produce a table that shows each advertising expenditure value as a percentage of each sales value. So, for instance, the first cell will show £2,000 as a percentage of £60,000.

Sales revenue £000	Advertising expediture £000
60	2
70	6
80	6
90	13
100	26
110	14
120	13
130	10
140	3
150	3

3. Using the table you created in Question 1, produce a third column that represents the percentages that each month's sales make up of total sales. Comment on your findings.

4. Using the data below present a table that contains a percentage figure for each sales figure as a percentage of total sales, and a percentage figure for each advertising expenditure figure as a percentage of total advertising expenditure. Comment on your findings.

Sales revenue £000	Advertising expenditure £000
115	12
122	14
132	16
142	18
152	18
162	22
172	24
220	45
310	56
290	46

5 Using your answer from Question 3 and the data below, present a table which shows costs as a percentage of sales and comment on your answer.

Month	Cost of goods £000
January	132
February	145
March	105
April	145
May	145
June	155
July	160
August	100
September	150
October	175
November	198
December	158

6 Plot the following data in a simple bar chart.

Month	Sales value £000
January	380
February	400
March	280
April	320
May	300
June	320
July	330
August	200
September	300
October	340
November	380
December	300

7 Use the data from July to December in the table in Question 6 to produce a pie chart. Show the data labels on the pie chart and highlight December.

8. Using the data below, plot Advertising as a percentage of total advertising against Sales as a percentage of total sales using a composite bar chart.

Sales revenue £000	Advertising expenditure £000	Advertising as percentage of total	Sales as percentage of total
115	12	4.4	6.3
122	14	5.2	6.7
132	16	5.9	7.3
142	18	6.6	7.8
152	18	6.6	8.4
162	22	8.1	8.9
172	24	8.9	9.5
220	45	16.6	12.1
310	56	20.7	17.1
290	46	17.0	16.0
1,817 Total	271 Total		

9. Using the table below, create a line chart that shows the relationship between sales and advertising.

Sales revenue £000	Advertising expenditure £000
115	12
122	14
132	16
142	18
152	18
162	22
172	24
220	45
310	56
290	46

Answers

1

Month	Sales value £000
January	380
February	400
March	280
April	320
May	300
June	320
July	330
August	200
September	300
October	340
November	380
December	300

Sales at Cleary car body workshop 2018

2

Sales revenue £000	Advertising expediture £000	Advertising as percentage of sales
60	2	3.3
70	6	8.6
80	6	7.5
90	13	14.4
100	26	26.0
110	14	12.7
120	13	10.8
130	10	7.7
140	3	2.1
150	3	2.0

Advertising as a percentage of sales

3

Month	Sales value £000	Sales as a percentage of total sales
January	380	9.9
February	400	10.4
March	280	7.3
April	320	8.3
May	300	7.8
June	320	8.3
July	330	8.6
August	200	5.2
September	300	7.8
October	340	8.8
November	380	9.9
December	300	7.8
Sales total	3,850	

Advertising sales as a percentage of total sales

4

Sales revenue £000	Advertising expenditure £000	Advertising as a percentage of total	Sales as a percentage of total
115	12	4.4	6.3
122	14	5.2	6.7
132	16	5.9	7.3
142	18	6.6	7.8
152	18	6.6	8.4
162	22	8.1	8.9
172	24	8.9	9.5
220	45	16.6	12.1
310	56	20.7	17.1
290	46	17.0	16.0
1,817	271		
Total	*Total*		

Comparison of relative percentages of sales and advertising expenditure

This table allows us to see the relationship between sales and advertising expenditure in a clearer way. In this case, sales and advertising expenditures as a percentage of their respective totals are close. For instance, when advertising is high as a percentage of total advertising expenditure the corresponding sales figure is high as a percentage of the total. The same is true when the figures are low for advertising as a percentage of total advertising expenditure since the corresponding percentage for sales is low as a percentage of total sales.

5

Month	Sales value £000	Cost of goods £000	Cost as a percentage of sales
January	380	132	34.7
February	400	145	36.3
March	280	105	37.5
April	320	145	45.3
May	300	145	48.3
June	320	155	48.4
July	330	160	48.5
August	200	100	50.0
September	300	150	50.0
October	340	175	51.5
November	380	198	52.1
December	300	158	52.7

Comparison of relative percentages of costs to sales

This table allows the Managing Director to see that costs are becoming larger in comparison to sales. This could be due to prices rising or it could be due to poor cost control by managers. Regardless of the cause, it highlights the issue of rising costs.

6

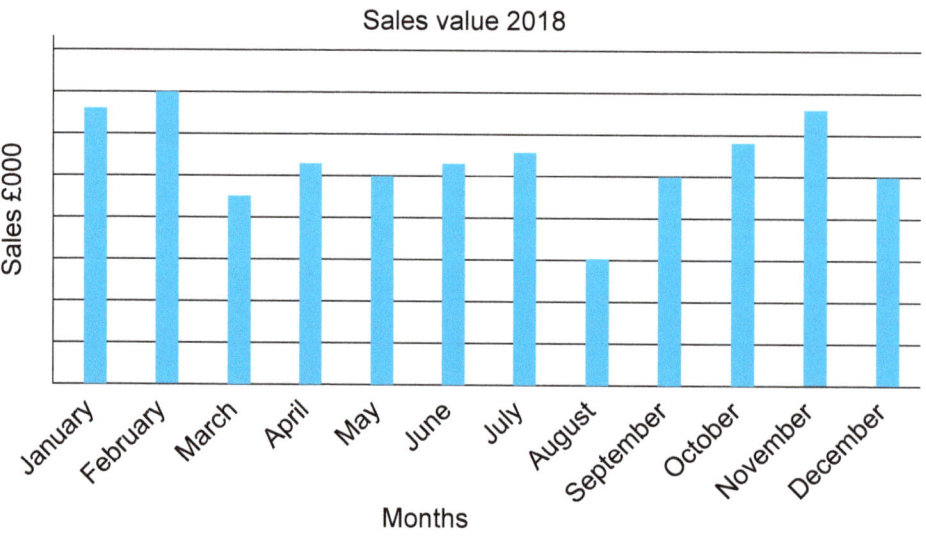

7

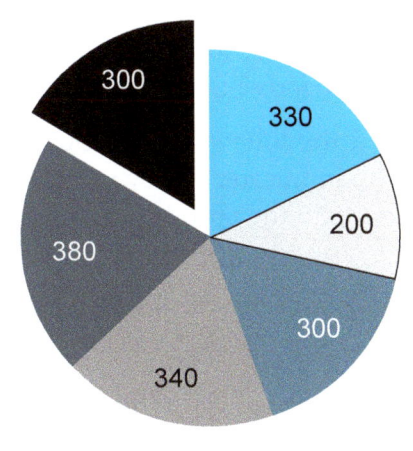

8

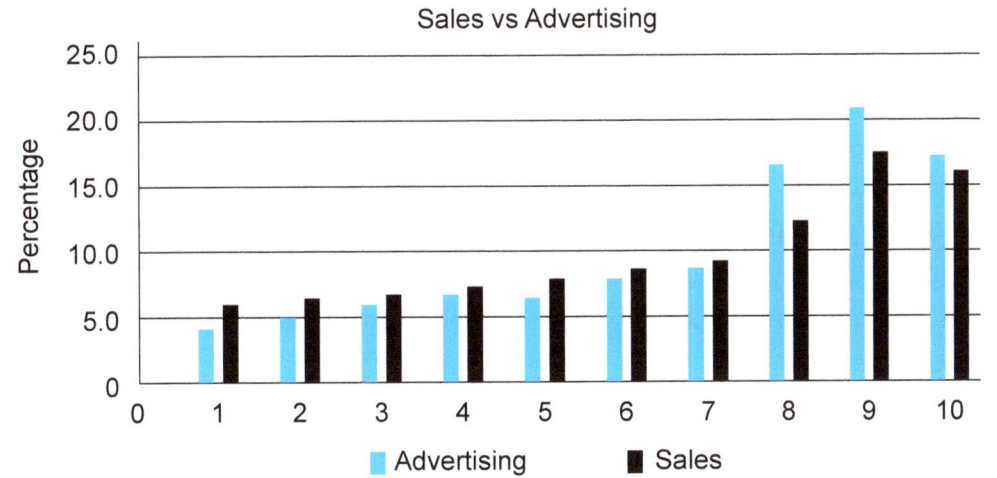

9

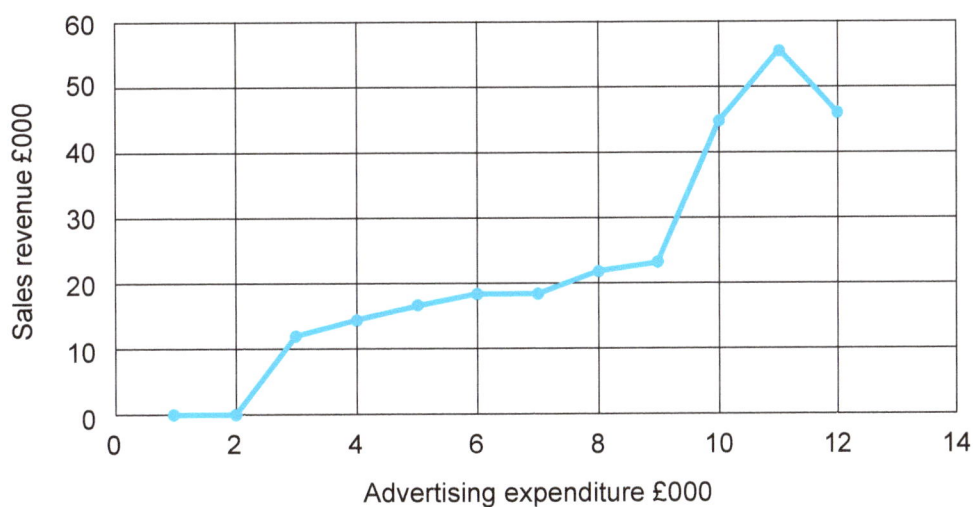

8.6 Progress questions

1. Using the following information create a table for the production of widgets at Widgets Plc over the period of a year that shows quarterly but also total production.

   During 2018 Widget Plc produced the following quantities of widgets according to the company's production department: in quarter 1 they produced 50,000 units, in quarter 2 they produced 45,000 units, in quarter 3 they produced 65,000 units, and in quarter 4 they produced 75,000 units.

2. Using the data in Question 1 show in a table the various percentages of total production that each quarter makes up over the year.

3. Guya Rum is a small retailer of rum to tourists on a tiny Caribbean island. The company's owner believes that there is a relationship between the company's sales of rum and the number of tourists visiting the island. Using the following data, generate a table that clearly shows the relationship between the two sets of figures. Use percentages to aid your analysis.

   Guya Rum sold the following during the summer of 2019: week 1 £25,000, week 2 £26,500, week 3 £27,800, week 4 £29,000, week 5 £25,000, week 6 £22,000, week 7 £31,000, week 8 £29,000, week 9 £31,000, week 10 £33,000.
   Tourist numbers during this period were as follows: week 1 11,000, week 2 11,700, week 3 12,500, week 4 13,600, week 5 11,200, week 6 12,200, week 7 14,000, week 8 13,800, week 9 14,050, week 10 16,000.

4. Read the following information about companies A and B.

   In 2017, company A had revenue of £800,000 from selling widgets and £205,000 from selling plogs. In 2018, company A had a revenue of £750,00 from selling widgets and £550,000 from selling plogs.

   In 2017, company B had revenue of £600,000 from selling widgets and £305,000 from selling plogs. In 2018, company B had revenue of £650,00 from selling widgets and £50,000 from selling plogs.

   Create a suitable table to show these results in a clearer way, and comment on the results.

5. Produce suitable diagrams to illustrate all of the data in Questions 1 to 4.

Chapter 9
Creating information and the measures of centrality

9.1 Introduction
9.2 Information
9.3 Introducing the three measures of centrality
9.4 Strengths and weaknesses of the measures of centrality
9.5 Review questions
9.6 Progress questions

9.1 Introduction

This chapter looks at how data is turned into information and introduces three very important statistical measures that are widely used in business. These statistical tools help to convey information to decision makers, and the chapter finishes by looking at their relative strengths and weaknesses.

9.2 Information

Data are observations which are collected and left unprocessed. Information is obtained by processing the data using a mathematical or statistical technique.

Example

A manager of a large car park company visits thirty small car parks in London and records the number of cars in each car park in a table (see Table 9.1). This is data.

10	50	30
20	50	60
30	40	40
30	40	50
30	50	40
40	20	80
50	10	50
60	30	120
80	60	40
60	50	90

Table 9.1 Raw data, unprocessed observations

If you look at the data in Table 9.1, it is difficult to get any meaningful understanding about the observations. What the manager needs to do is process the data to turn it into information. A very simplistic way of doing this is to place the data in an ordered arrangement, for instance, lowest to highest. Such a presentation is shown in Table 9.2, and is called an ordered array.

10	40	50
10	40	50
20	40	60
20	40	60
30	40	60
30	50	60
30	50	80
30	50	80
30	50	90
40	50	120

Table 9.2 Ordered array: ascending array

Now if you look at the data you will see that some patterns are starting to emerge. First, the extremities of the range of data are clearer to detect: the values at either end of the data array are 10 and 120 cars. You should also observe some data bunching; that is, where some observations occur more frequently than others within this array. The simple process of creating an array has therefore generated information. However, by itself this is a simplistic approach to data analysis.

The 'next steps' would to be to create a tally table and then a frequency table.

In Table 9.3 the manager has taken the data from Table 9.2 and created a tally table. This is produced by searching the data and marking a slanting line (/) every time an observation occurs. Every fifth observation of a value is marked by striking through the four slanted lines with a horizontal line to create a 'gate" (////).

Cars	Tally
10	//
20	//
30	////
40	//// /
50	//// //
60	////
80	//
90	/
120	/

Table 9.3 Tally table

The benefit of the tally table is that it highlights some potential simple patterns in the data collected. In Table 9.3 it gives a visual representation of the data bunching between 30 and 60 cars, and illustrates that as we move to the lower and higher extremities of the values observed there are fewer and fewer of these observations.

An alternative presentation is an enhancement of the tally table, called a frequency table. The frequency is simply the number of times an observation occurs. Using the tally in Table 9.3, a frequency and tally table can been produced (Table 9.4).

Cars	Tally	Frequency
10	//	2
20	//	2
30	////	5
40	//// /	6
50	//// //	7
60	////	4
80	//	2
90	/	1
120	/	1

Table 9.4 Tally and frequency table

The frequency table is not just an alternative way of presenting the tally of the observations, but it is also something that can be used for further statistical analysis.

Practice question 1

A large supermarket chain is looking at the number of returns that individual customer service team members are dealing with per hour with a view to possibly recruiting more team members. The data below comprises the number of customer service interactions per member of staff observed in 10 stores over 4 hours on 1 August 2018. Use this data to create a tally table and frequency table and identify any patterns that you notice.

12	15	18	9
14	17	16	15
15	18	6	16
16	16	12	22
18	20	25	21
22	12	24	14
3	24	23	5
5	16	19	6
19	18	17	14
12	22	6	17

9.3 Introducing the three measures of centrality

We saw in the previous section that raw unprocessed data could be turned into information using quite a simple process. This section will look at further simple mathematical operations to produce summary measures to represent a data set. The three measures we are going to explore are known as measures of centrality, or in everyday terminology as averages. They are the mode, the median and the mean.

The mode

The mode is the value that appears most frequently in a data set.

Example

1, 2, 3, 4, 4, 5, 6, 6, 6

The mode in this small data set is 6 because it occurs three times, which is more than any other.

Practice question 2

Identify the mode for the data in Table 9.5.

12.0
12.2
12.3
13.4
13.8
13.2
13.3
13.4
12.3
12.5
12.3
12.4
13.0
13.2
15.0

Table 9.5 Observations of the weight of sacks of chemicals at a fertiliser plant in kgs

The median

The median is the value that splits a data set into two equal parts.

> *Example*
>
> 3, 1, 5, 4, 6, 7, 8, 6, 9
>
> The first step in finding the median is to place the data into ascending order.
>
> 3, 1, 5, 4, 6, 7, 8, 6, 9
>
> is placed into an ascending ordered array:
>
> 1, 3, 4, 5, 6, 6, 7, 8, 9
>
> Once the data has been arranged, identify the value that splits the data set into two. In this case there are nine observations and the median can be easily identified, as shown in Figure 9.1, where the top line represents the ordered array of data observations.
>
> The middle value in this data set (once placed into an ordered array) is the fifth value, which if you count from left to right is 6 and therefore the value of the median is 6.

1	3	4	5	6	6	7	8	9
				Median value				
4 observations to left				5th observation (middle value)	4 observations to right			

Figure 9.1 The median

An alternative way to obtain the median for a data set is to use the simple formula below to identify the median position:

$$\frac{(n + 1)}{2}$$

where n is the number of observations in the data set.

So, for the data in the example, the median value is $(9 + 1)/2 = 5$, which is the fifth value in the array.

The median is quite easy to obtain with an odd number of observations in a data set so the use of the formula may not seem to offer an advantage. However, where the number of observations is even the problem changes because the middle value is not so clear.

Example

Look at the following data set (it is already ordered):

1, 4, 5, 6, 8, 11, 12, 13, 15, 18

Applying the formula for identifying the median value:

$$\frac{(10 + 1)}{2}$$

so the median is the $5\frac{1}{2}$th value; in other words, a value that lies between the 5th and 6th value. Where this situation occurs, take the two values on either side of this middle value, the 5th and 6th in this example, add them together and divide by two:

$$\frac{(8 + 11)}{2} = 9.5$$

Therefore the median is 9.5.

Practice question 3

Calculate the median for the data in Table 9.5.

The mean

Strictly speaking, this measure is the arithmetic mean but it is usually just called the mean. When people talk about the average value, they are usually referring to the mean.

The mean is obtained by summing all the values in the data set and dividing by the number of observations. The following example illustrates the calculation of the mean.

Example

Look at the data below:

1, 2, 3, 4, 5, 6, 7, 8, 9

The first step in calculating the mean is to sum these observations, which comes to 45. The next step is to divide by the number of observations, of which there are 9.

$$\frac{45}{9} = 5$$

therefore the mean is 5.

Practice question 4

Calculate the mean for the data in Table 9.5 to 2 decimal places.

Practice question 5

Calculate the three measures of central tendency for the data in Practice Question 1.

9.4 Strengths and weaknesses of the measures of centrality

Each of the three measures above have strengths and weaknesses but despite their relative strengths and weaknesses they all have their use in business and beyond.

The mode

The strength of the mode is that it is easy to obtain and understand.

Look again at the data in Table 9.2.

10	40	50
10	40	50
20	40	60
20	40	60
30	40	60
30	50	60
30	50	80
30	50	80
30	50	90
40	50	120

Table 9.2 Ordered array: ascending array

The mode is 50 cars as it is the most frequently occurring observation, something that is relatively easy to identify.

The first disadvantage of the mode is that it only represents the most frequency occurring value and as such is not much use for representing the whole of a data set.

The next problem for the mode is that there can be more than one of them.

Example

3, 3, 4, 5, 6, 7, 8, 9, 4, 5, 6, 7, 5, 3

There are two modes in this data set: 3 and 5.

An advantage of the mode is that it is unaffected by extreme values, that is 'outliers'. So, for instance, if the last value in Table 9.2 was 900 rather than 120 the value for the mode would still be 50.

The median

The strength of the median is that it represents the centre of the data set and is therefore unaffected by extreme values.

Example

The median for the data in Table 9.2 is 45.

This is obtained by first working out the position of the median value.

$$\frac{(30 + 1)}{2} = 15.5\text{th value}$$

Then the mode is calculated by adding the 15th value and the 16th value, and dividing by 2:

$$\frac{(40 + 50)}{2} = 45 \text{ cars}$$

This seems to provide a better representation of the data in Table 9.2 than the mode because it tells us about the centre of the data set. Look back to the tally in Table 9.3 and you can see that the data was bunched around this value. But the median, although useful, does have its failings in representing the complete data set because it only tells us about the centre.

However, the median does have one advantage over the other measures in that it can be used with ordinal (ranked) data. Ordinal data consists of information that can be categorised and ordered, but for which there is no quantifiable relationship between categories. Examples of ordinal data include one- to five-star ratings of hotels and indicators of customer satisfaction.

The mean

The main advantage of the mean is that it represents all the values in a data set. That is, each observation in the data set contributes to the calculation of the measure. It is this characteristic that makes the mean such an important measure and why it is used in the further statistical analysis of data.

Example

The mean for the data in Table 9.2 is obtained by adding up all the values and dividing by the number of observations.

The sum of all the values comes to 1,410.

The number of observations is 30, therefore the mean is:

$$\frac{(1,410)}{30} = 47 \text{ cars}$$

The disadvantage of the mean is that it is affected by extreme values, that is outliers. To illustrate the point look at the example below.

Example

Look at the two data sets:

(a) 10, 10, 10, 10, 10, 10, 10, 10, 10, 10

and

(b) 1, 1, 1, 1, 1, 1, 1, 1, 1, 91

If you calculate the mean for these two data sets, you find that both are 10. This is because they both have 10 observations and both sum to 100, giving 100/10 = 10.

But of course, the data sets look very different. They have the same mean because the unusual outlier in data set (b) of 91 is so large.

Example

If the last value in Table 9.2 was changed from 120 to 900, the mean would change from 47 cars, as calculated above.

New total = 2,190

Number of observations = 30

Therefore, the mean is now: 2,190/30 = 73 cars

$$\frac{(2,100)}{30} = 73 \text{ cars}$$

Once again, an outlier has heavily influenced the mean. The mean is particularly susceptible to outliers in small data sets, particularly when the outliers are quite large relative to the other values in the data set. One way around this problem is to trim the data set before the mean is calculated by excluding the outliers, which can be either unusually large or small values.

Example

Calculate the trimmed mean for the data sets below by excluding outliers.

(a) 10, 10, 10, 10, 10, 10, 10, 10, 10, 10

(b) 1, 1, 1, 1, 1, 1, 1, 1, 1, 91

Data set (a) would remain unchanged while 91 would be removed from data set (b).

Therefore, the mean for data set (b) would now be based upon the nine 1s, which of course would provide a mean of 1. This value would surely seem to represent data set (b) better.

An alternative way to help mitigate the consequences of the mean being impacted upon by outliers would be to identify a 'measure of spread', but this is beyond the remit of this book.

9.5 Review questions

1 Use the following data to construct a frequency and tally table.

26	55
22	72
85	56
55	38
63	55
28	26
27	65
32	22
45	72
45	27
36	38
45	45
55	36

2 Obtain the three measures of centrality for the data below.

26	32	33	45
22	45	63	72
85	45	56	52
55	42	29	38
63	45	62	45
28	55	45	36
27	58	65	

3 Obtain the three measures of centrality for the data below.

32	19	33
56	18	63
15	56	56
55	21	29
63	21	62
28	23	45
27	58	

4 The data show the period in days that stock is held in 24 pubs belonging to a beer brewer. Obtain the three measures of centrality for this data and comment on your findings.

46	48	47	43
45	50	56	52
55	42	29	38
63	12	22	85
28	55	41	21
21	33	21	55

5 The data show the number of employees per medium-sized supermarket in the south-east of England for a small supermarket chain. Obtain the three measures of centrality for this data and comment on your findings.

65	48	46	40
75	50	56	52
89	92	29	50
63	101	57	85
41	55	41	65

126

Answers

1

Observations	Tally	Frequency
22	//	2
26	//	2
27	//	2
28	/	1
32	/	1
36	//	2
38	//	2
45	////	4
55	////	4
56	/	1
63	/	1
65	/	1
72	//	2
85	/	1

Tally and frequency table

2   Mean   47
    Mode   45
    Median   45

3   Mean   39
    Mode   56
    Median   32.5

4   Mean   42
    Mode   55
    Median   44

There are two extreme periods for stock being held, suggesting the possibilities of inefficiency and efficiency within two of the pubs. The mean is 42 days and the most frequently occurring observation is 55 days. 50% of the observations are below 44 and 50% are above.

5   Mean   60
    Mode   65
    Median   55.5

The data contain one notable figure over 100, with three observations being quite far from the mean of 60. The most frequently occurring observation was 65 employees and 50% of the observations were below 55.5 and 50% above.

9.6 Progress questions

1   Use the following data to produce a tally and frequency table.

15	22	23
21	25	26
19	24	21
22	28	18
18	24	19
22	29	
19	17	
17	18	
16	19	
18	24	

2   Calculate the three measures of centrality for the data set in Question 1.

3   Calculate the three measures of centrality for the data below.

31	86	85
32	59	56
26	28	63
85	35	64
65	68	78
35	79	52
45	81	45

4 Calculate the three measures of centrality for the data below and comment on the relative values of the three measures.

71	65	69
60	69	62
68	67	63
140	57	65
62	59	65
72	68	64

5 Identify the best measure of central of tendency for the following problems:
   (a) A shoe manufacturer wishes to know the average shoe size for manufacturing purposes.
   (b) A carpet manufacturer needs to know the average price of its competitor's heavy underlay.
   (c) A researcher needs to know the average rank, in terms of competence, of a sample of clients who have a particular characteristic.

6 Imagine you are a high-flying executive. You have the choice of working for two employers. The median wage for employer 1 is £15,000, while for employer 2 it is £19,000. The mean salary for each is £22,000. Which company would you select?

7 How can the main weakness of the mean be overcome?

Chapter 10
Test your knowledge

This chapter consolidates what you have previously learnt in class and self-study. You should spend an hour on Paper 5 attempting the questions, before checking your answers.

10.1 Paper 5

INSTRUCTIONS:

1. This paper comprises 6 questions. All questions should be attempted
2. Clear presentation and derivation of answers is required
3. The number of marks is indicated at the end of each question
4. This assessment has 34 marks available in total

QUESTION 1

(a) Calculate the profit share of each partner for the following partnerships:
   (i) A, B and C share profits in the ratio of 4:8:2. Total profit is £560,000.

A	
B	
C	

   (ii) X, Y and Z share profits in the ratio of 5:4:6. Total profit is £495,000.

X	
Y	
Z	

   (2 marks)

(b) Calculate the following:
   (i) 19 as a percentage of 304.
   (ii) £19.95 as a percentage of £399.00.
   (iii) The difference between £770 and £924 as a percentage of £770.

   (3 marks)

(c) The following marks were gained out of 100 by 9 students in their final exams:

56; 32; 72; 76; 46; 60; 63; 42; 57.

What was the average mark for this exam?

(2 marks)

(Total: 7 marks)

QUESTION 2

(a) A watch repairer works a basic 35-hour week at an hourly rate of £12.50. If overtime is worked, it is paid at time and a half. How much would he be paid *in total* in a week in which he worked his normal hours plus 11 hours overtime?

(2 marks)

(b) Sally sells advertising space. She is paid a salary of £7,500 per year. On top of this she is paid a commission on the amount of sales she makes, which is calculated as follows:

She receives commission of 4% on the value of all sales up to £400,000;
She receives commission of 10% on sales greater than £400.000.

Calculate Sally's total pay in a year in which she sells £750,000 worth of advertising space.

(3 marks)

(Total: 5 marks)

QUESTION 3

(a) What is the price you would pay for a £8,800 car if a discount of 12½% were to be applied?

(2 marks)

(b) Two shops are selling identical bottles of perfume. The usual price charged by both shops is £27.50 per bottle, but today each shop has a special offer:
  Shop A is offering three bottles for the price of two;
  Shop B is saying that if I buy three bottles I will have a 20% discount.

I want to buy 3 bottles at the cheapest total price, so whose offer should I accept?
(Show all your workings)

(3 marks)

(Total: 5 marks)

QUESTION 4

(a) I went to France for a week and, before I left, bought €5,000, paying in £s. The exchange rate was €1.18 for £1.

At the end of the week I had €1,700 left, and when I returned to the UK I exchanged this amount for £s at the new exchange rate €1.11 for £1.

How much did my trip to France cost me *in £s*?

(2 marks)

(b) Mike invests £15,000 into a savings account for one year. The compound interest rate is 6% per annum, which is paid into the account every 6 months.

Calculate the value of this investment at the end of one year.

(2 marks)

(Total: 4 marks)

QUESTION 5

A company buys a fleet of 20 cars, each costing £17,250. It is decided that the capital cost will be written off in equal instalments over 5 years, after which the cars will have no scrap value.

Calculate the value of the fleet of cars after the end of year 3.

(Total: 6 marks)

QUESTION 6

Read the following information on two consulting companies, A and B.

In 2017, consulting company A had income of £200,000 from marketing clients and £125,000 from financial clients.

The 2017 figures for consulting company B were £300,000 from marketing clients and £150,000 from financial clients.

In 2018 the figures for A were £350,000 from marketing clients and £200,000 from financial clients, while B's figures were £325,000 from marketing clients and £250,000 from financial clients.

Create a suitable table to show these results in a clearer way, and comment on the results.

(Total: 7 marks)

10.2 Paper 5 answers

QUESTION 1

(a) Calculate the profit share of each partner for the following partnerships:

   (i) A, B and C share profits in the ratio of 4:8:2. Total profit is £560,000.

A	
B	
C	

   (ii) X, Y and Z share profits in the ratio of 5:4:6. Total profit is £495,000.

X	
Y	
Z	

(2 marks)

(b) Calculate the following:
   (i) 19 as a percentage of 304.
   (ii) £19.95 as a percentage of £399.00.
   (iii) The difference between £770 and £924 as a percentage of £770.

   (3 marks)

(c) The following marks were gained out of 100 by 9 students in their final exams:

   56; 32; 72; 76; 46; 60; 63; 42; 57.

   What was the average mark for this exam?

   (2 marks)
   (Total: 7 marks)

Answers

(a) (i)

A	£160,000
B	£320,000
C	£80,000

(ii)

X	£165,000
Y	£132,000
Z	£198,000

(b) (i) 6.25%
   (ii) 5%
   (iii) 20%

(c) 56%

QUESTION 2

(a) A watch repairer works a basic 35-hour week at an hourly rate of £12.50. If overtime is worked, it is paid at time and a half. How much would he be paid *in total* in a week in which he worked his normal hours plus 11 hours overtime?

   (2 marks)

(b) Sally sells advertising space. She is paid a salary of £7,500 per year. On top of this she is paid a commission on the amount of sales she makes, which is calculated as follows:
   She receives commission of 4% on the value of all sales up to £400,000;
   She receives commission of 10% on sales greater than £400,000.

   Calculate Sally's total pay in a year in which she sells £750,000 worth of advertising space.

   (3 marks)
   (Total: 5 marks)

Answers

(a) £643.75

(b) £58,500

QUESTION 3

(a) What is the price you would pay for a £8,800 car if a discount of 12½% were to be applied?

(2 marks)

(b) Two shops are selling identical bottles of perfume. The usual price charged by both shops is £27.50 per bottle, but today each shop has a special offer:

Shop A is offering three bottles for the price of two;

Shop B is saying that if I buy three bottles I will have a 20% discount.

I want to buy 3 bottles at the cheapest total price, so whose offer should I accept?
(Show all your workings)

(3 marks)

(Total: 5 marks)

Answers

(a) £7,700

(b) Shop A £55; Shop B £66. Therefore Shop A is the better option by £11.

QUESTION 4

(a) I went to France for a week and, before I left, bought €5,000, paying in £s. The exchange rate was €1.18 for £1.

At the end of the week I had €1,700 left, and when I returned to the UK I exchanged this amount for £s at the new exchange rate €1.11 for £1.

How much did my trip to France cost me *in £s*?

(2 marks)

(b) Mike invests £15,000 into a savings account for one year. The compound interest rate is 6% per annum, which is paid into the account every 6 months.

Calculate the value of this investment at the end of one year.

(2 marks)

(Total: 4 marks)

Answers

(a) £2,705.76

(b) £15,913.50

QUESTION 5

A company buys a fleet of 20 cars, each costing £17,250. It is decided that the capital cost will be written off in equal instalments over 5 years, after which the cars will have no scrap value.

Calculate the value of the fleet of cars after the end of year 3.

(Total: 6 marks)

Answer

£138,000

QUESTION 6

Read the following information on two consulting companies, A and B.

In 2017, consulting company A had income of £200,000 from marketing clients and £125,000 from financial clients.

The 2017 figures for consulting company B were £300,000 from marketing clients and £150,000 from financial clients.

In 2018, the figures for A were £350,000 from marketing clients and £200,000 from financial clients, while B's figures were £325,000 from marketing clients and £250,000 from financial clients.

Create a suitable table to show these results in a clearer way, and comment on the results.

(Total: 7 marks)

Answers

Company A	MKT (000s)	FIN (000s)	Total	Company B	MKT (000s)	FIN (000s)	Total
2017	200	125	325	2017	300	150	450
2018	350	200	550	2018	325	250	575
Total	550	325	875	Total	625	400	1,025

(1) Company B's total income in the year 2017 is 38.46% greater than company A's in the same period.

(2) Company B's total income in the year 2018 is 4.55% greater than company A's in the same period.

(3) Over the two years, company B's total income is 17.14% greater than company A's in the same period.

Other valid comments are acceptable.

10.3 Paper 6

QUESTION 1

(a) Calculate the profit share of each partner for the following partnerships:

(i) A, B and C share profits in the ratio of 3:6:2. Total profit is £693,000.

A	
B	
C	

(ii) X, Y and Z share profits in the ratio of 7:3:4. Total profit is £495,000.

X	
Y	
Z	

(2 marks)

(b) Calculate the following:
(i) 17 as a percentage of 391.
(ii) £17.99 as a percentage of £899.50.
(iii) The difference between £365 and £500 as a percentage of £365.

(3 marks)

(c) The following marks were gained out of 100 by 11 students in their final exams:

56; 32; 72; 76; 46; 60; 63; 42; 57; 78; 33.

What was the average mark for this exam?

(2 marks)

(Total: 7 marks)

QUESTION 2

(a) A waiter works a basic 35-hour week at an hourly rate of £8. If overtime is worked, it is paid at time and a half. How much would he be paid *in total* in a week in which he worked his normal hours plus 11 hours overtime?

(2 marks)

(b) Sally sells advertising space. She is paid a salary of £6,500 per year. On top of this she is paid a commission on the amount of sales she makes, which is calculated as follows:

She receives commission of 4% on the value of all sales up to £400,000;
She receives commission of 10% on sales greater than £400.000.

Calculate Sally's total pay in a year in which she sells £900,000 worth of advertising space.

(3 marks)

(Total: 5 marks)

QUESTION 3

(a) What is the price you would pay for a £11,000 car if a discount of 6% were to be applied?

(2 marks)

(b) Two shops are selling identical bottles of perfume. The usual price charged by both shops is £30.00 per bottle, but today each shop has a special offer:

Shop A is offering three bottles for the price of two;

Shop B is saying that if I buy three bottles I will have a 20% discount.

I want to buy 3 bottles at the cheapest total price, so whose offer should I accept?
(Show all your workings)

(3 marks)

(Total: 5 marks)

QUESTION 4

(a) I went to France for a week and, before I left, bought €7,000, paying in £s (sterling). The exchange rate was €1.11 for £1.

At the end of the week I had €1,600 left, and when I returned to the UK I exchanged this amount for £s (sterling) at the new exchange rate €1.05 for £1.

How much did my trip to France cost me *in £s*?

(2 marks)

(b) Mike invests £17,000 into a savings account for one year. The compound interest rate is 4% per annum, which is paid into the account every 6 months.

Calculate the value of this investment at the end of one year.

(2 marks)

(Total: 4 marks)

QUESTION 5

A company buys a fleet of 15 cars, each costing £23,000. It is decided that the capital cost will be written off in equal instalments over 5 years, after which the cars will have no scrap value.

Calculate the value of the fleet of cars after the end of year 4.

(Total: 6 marks)

QUESTION 6

Read the following information on two consulting companies, A and B.

In 2017, consulting company A had income of £300,000 from marketing clients and £150,000 from financial clients.

The 2017 figures for consulting company B were £275,000 from marketing clients and £160,000 from financial clients.

In 2018, the figures for A were £250,000 from marketing clients and £160,000 from financial clients, while B's figures were £350,000 from marketing clients and £270,000 from financial clients.

Create a suitable table to show these results in a clearer way, and comment on the results.

(Total: 7 marks)

Chapter 11
Drawing charts using Excel

Although many of you will not be required to produce diagrams to the same standard as those in this book, students often ask how they can produce such high quality figures. For those of you who want to know, this chapter is a simple introduction.

The authors use the graphic capabilities of Microsoft Excel© to draw graphs and charts. There are of course other spreadsheet packages that provide similar functions, but we prefer this package.

The following text will guide you through the process of drawing charts using Excel's 'Recommended Chart' function. This function may not be available in some versions of Excel, but the procedure will be similar.

First, open Excel by clicking on the Excel icon on your desktop or selecting it from your Start menu.

Once opened the screen will look like this:

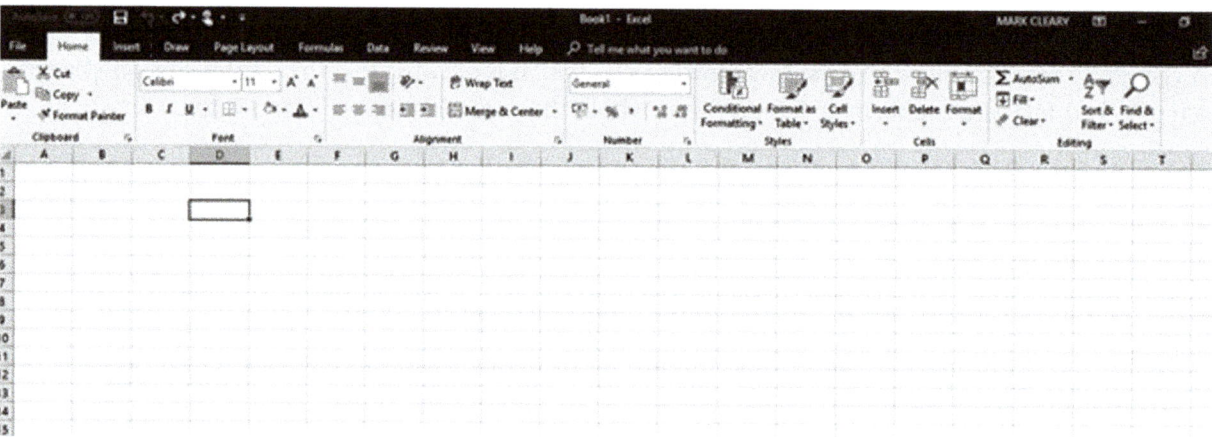

Used with permission from Microsoft.

We have used the data from Table 8.9 to demonstrate how to create charts. You can either enter the data manually or copy and paste it from the document containing it.

The Excel document then looks like this:

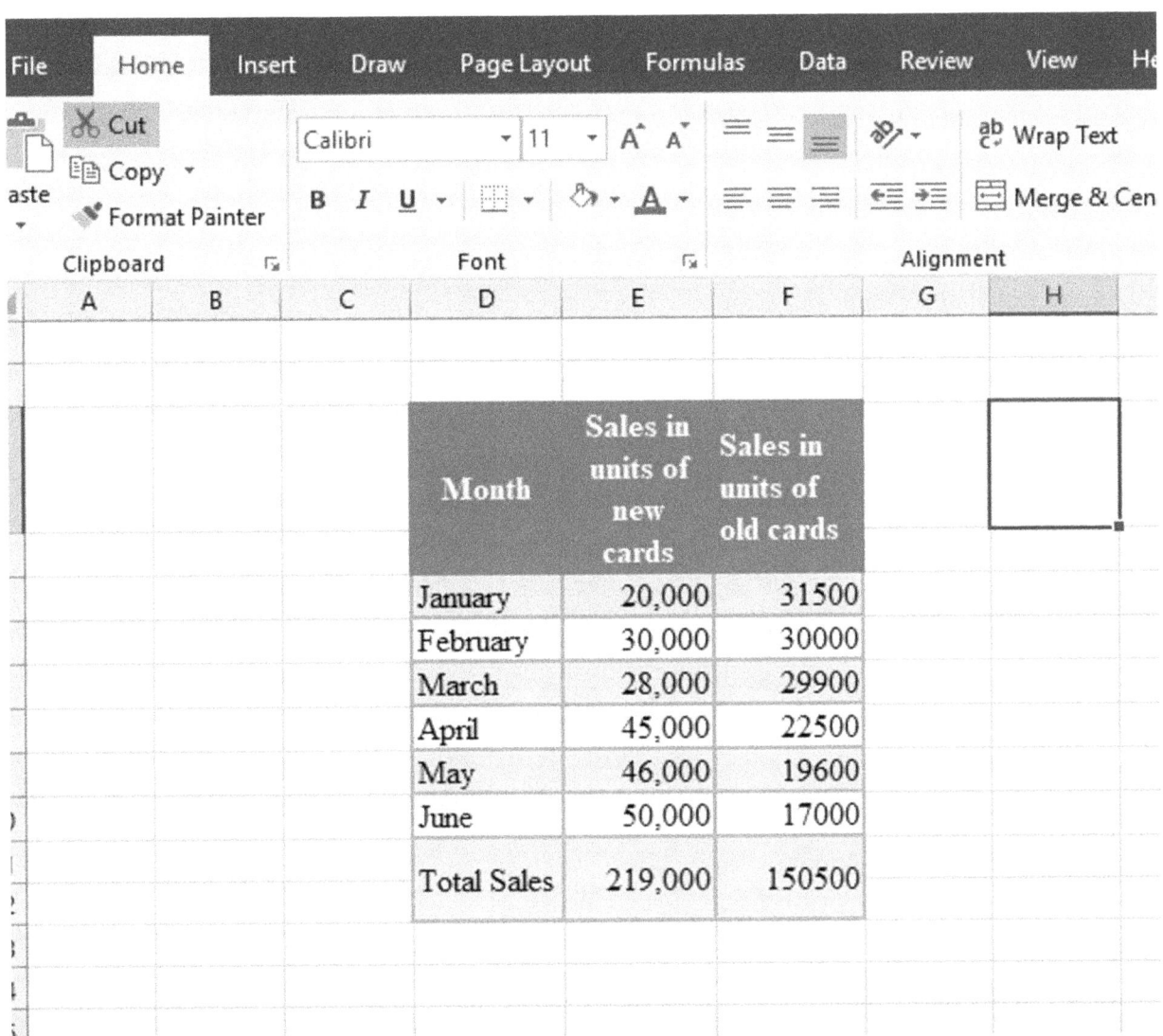

Used with permission from Microsoft.

Next, highlight the table you have created. You do this by placing the cross hair of your mouse on the top left-hand corner cell, which in this example has the label 'Month'. Once this is highlighted, depress the shift key on your computer and use the arrows on the keyboard to highlight the rest of the table keeping the shift key depressed. Once you have highlighted the area you wish to be plotted release the shift key. Alternatively, you can drag your mouse from top left to bottom right of the table, keeping the mouse button depressed.

The spreadsheet should now look like this:

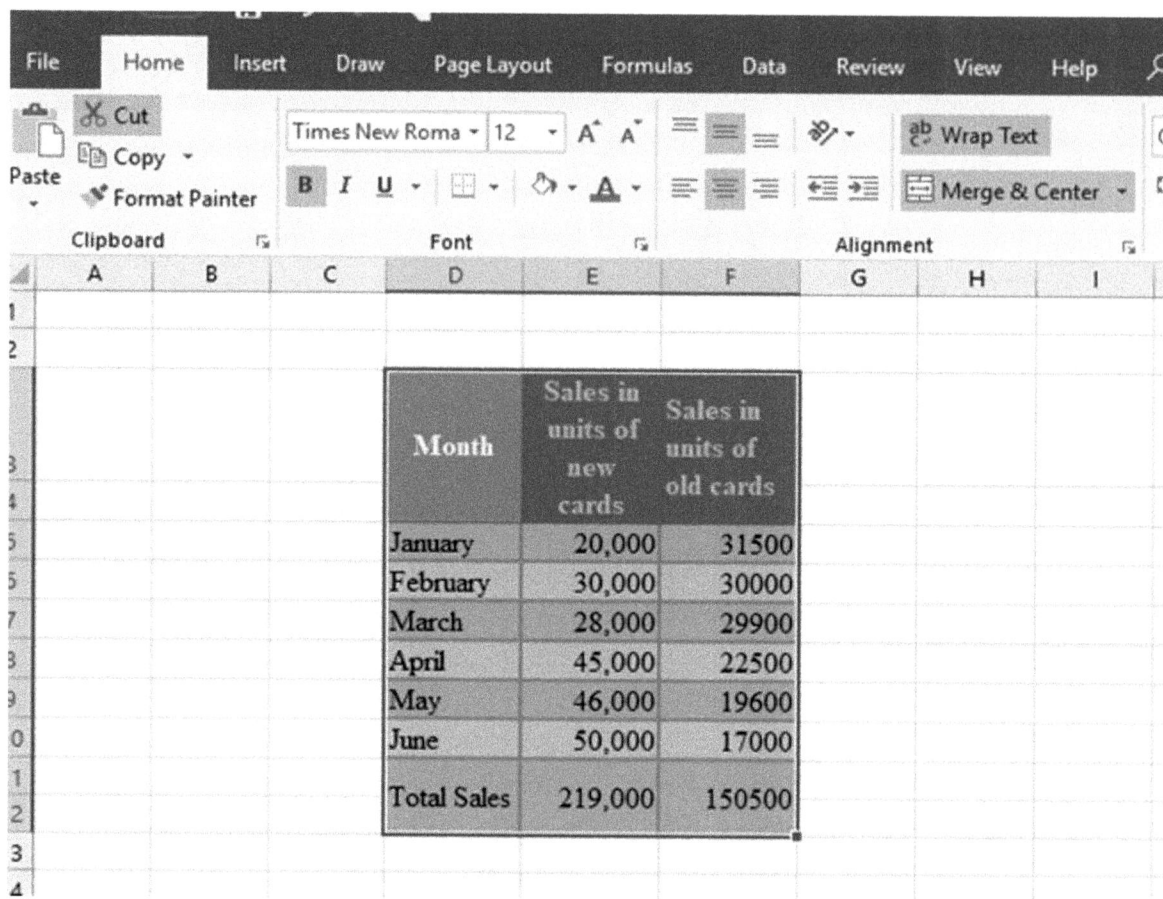

Used with permission from Microsoft.

Now, look at the top of the screen and click on the ribbon tab marked 'Insert'. The screen will now appear as:

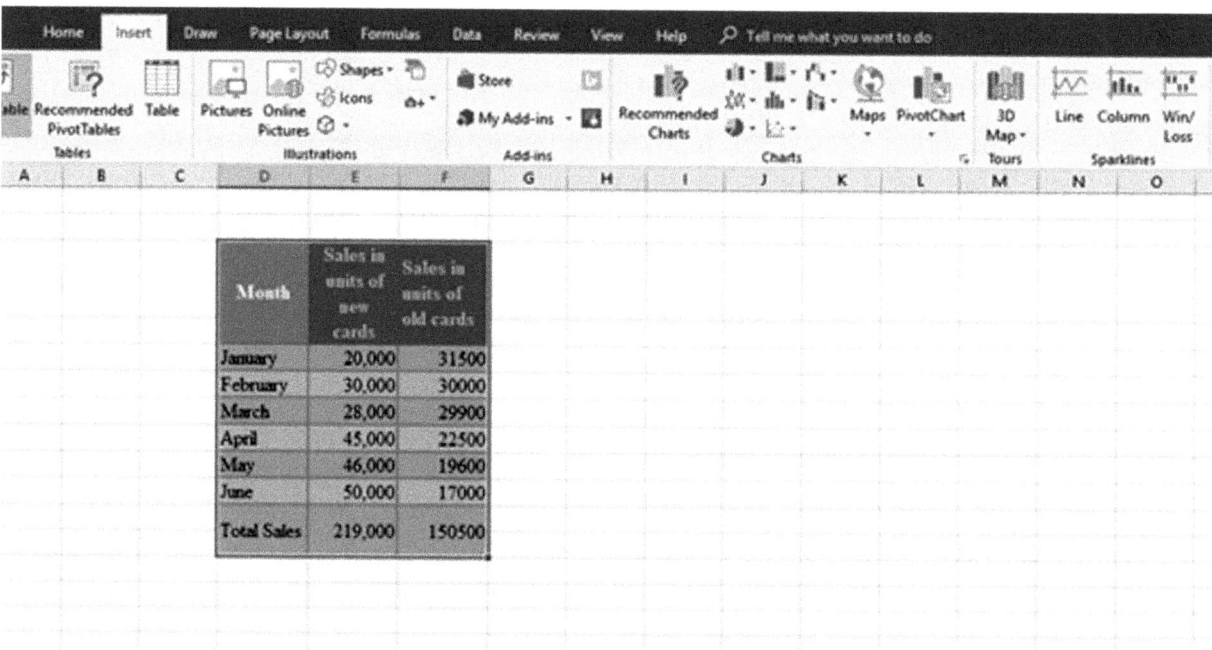

Used with permission from Microsoft.

Note that a new menu has appeared below the green ribbon at the top. Looking at the Charts section, Excels makes it easy to draw charts by recommending different types of diagrams. You can then customise the chart by changing colours, titles, labels, etc.

Click on the 'Recommended Charts' icon and the screen will change to:

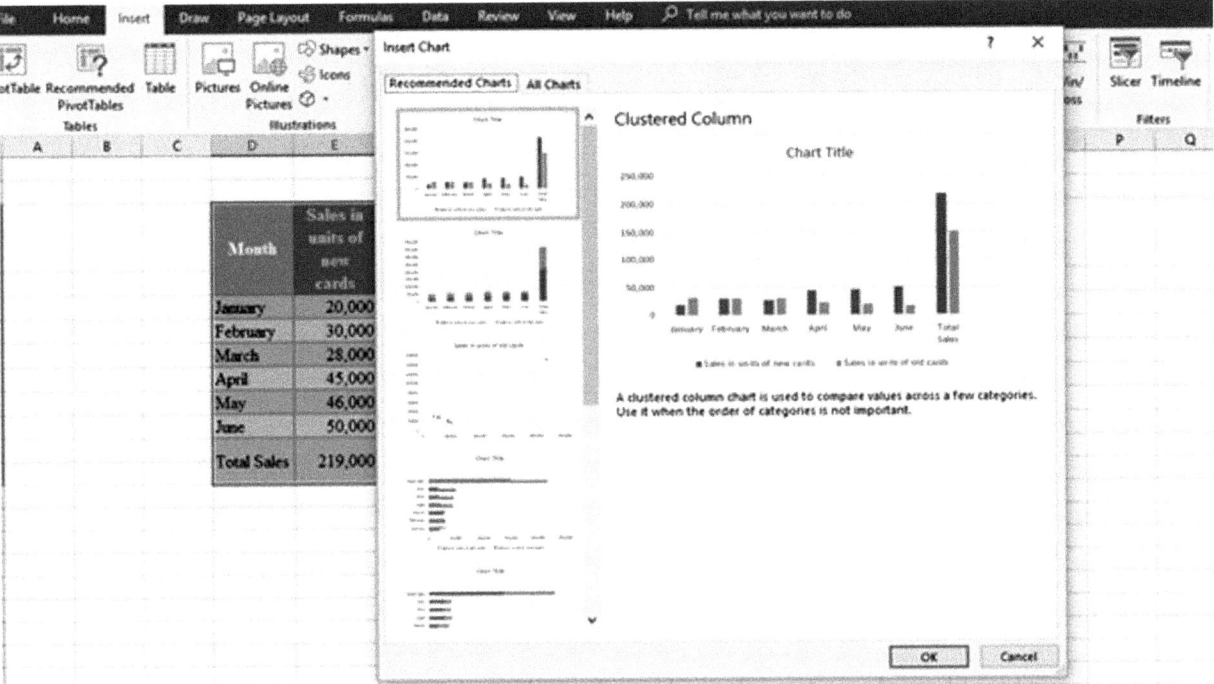

Used with permission from Microsoft.

In the centre of the screen is a dialog box which is divided into two panes. The main area is Excel's first attempt at meeting your needs. If you are happy with that chart, you can click OK, the box will disappear, and the chart will appear embedded in your diagram. Alternatively, you can look at the left-hand pane which shows previews of many other types of charts. To get a better view, just click on one and it will become the main chart in the right-hand pane of the dialog box. Again, if you click OK you have selected your chart type and the dialog box will close. So, if you accept the first chart offered by Excel and click on OK, the following screen appears.

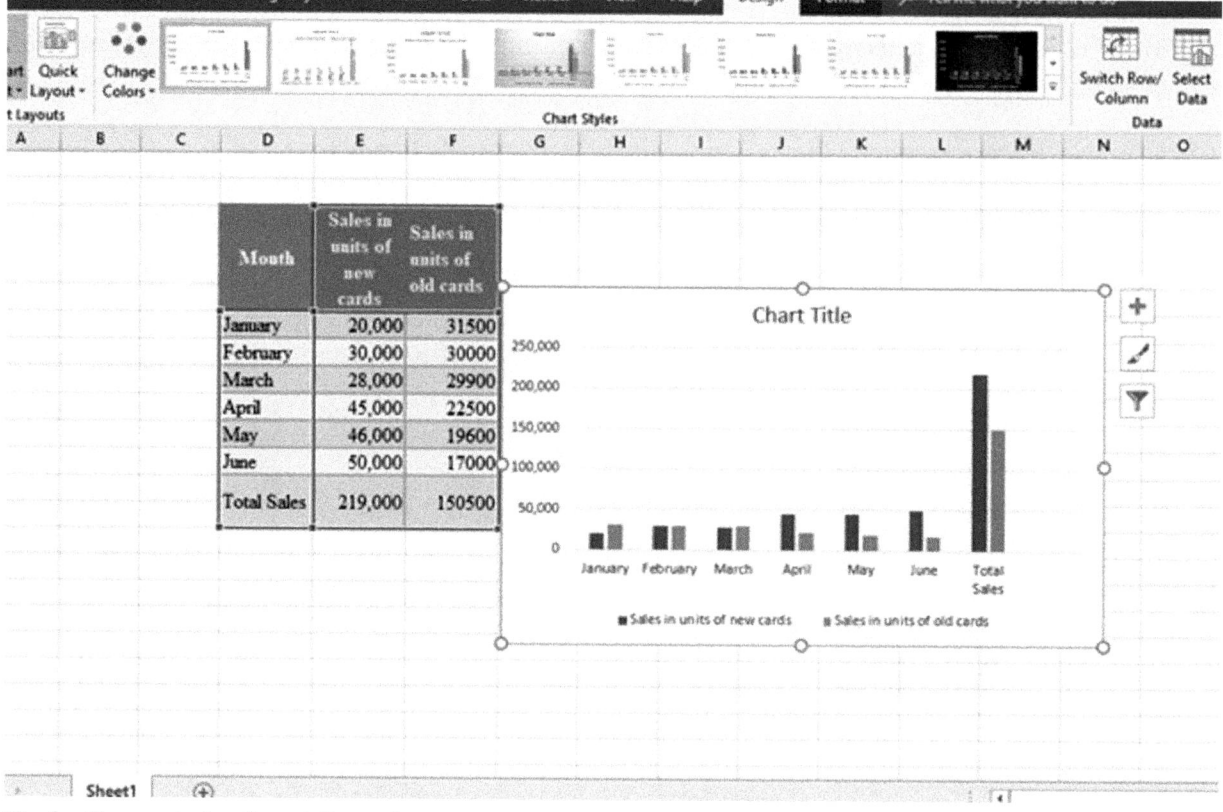

Used with permission from Microsoft.

At this point you can start to change colours or appearances to suit your presentation. You can change the chart title to a useful name by clicking on 'Chart Title' and editing the text, e.g. Card Sales.

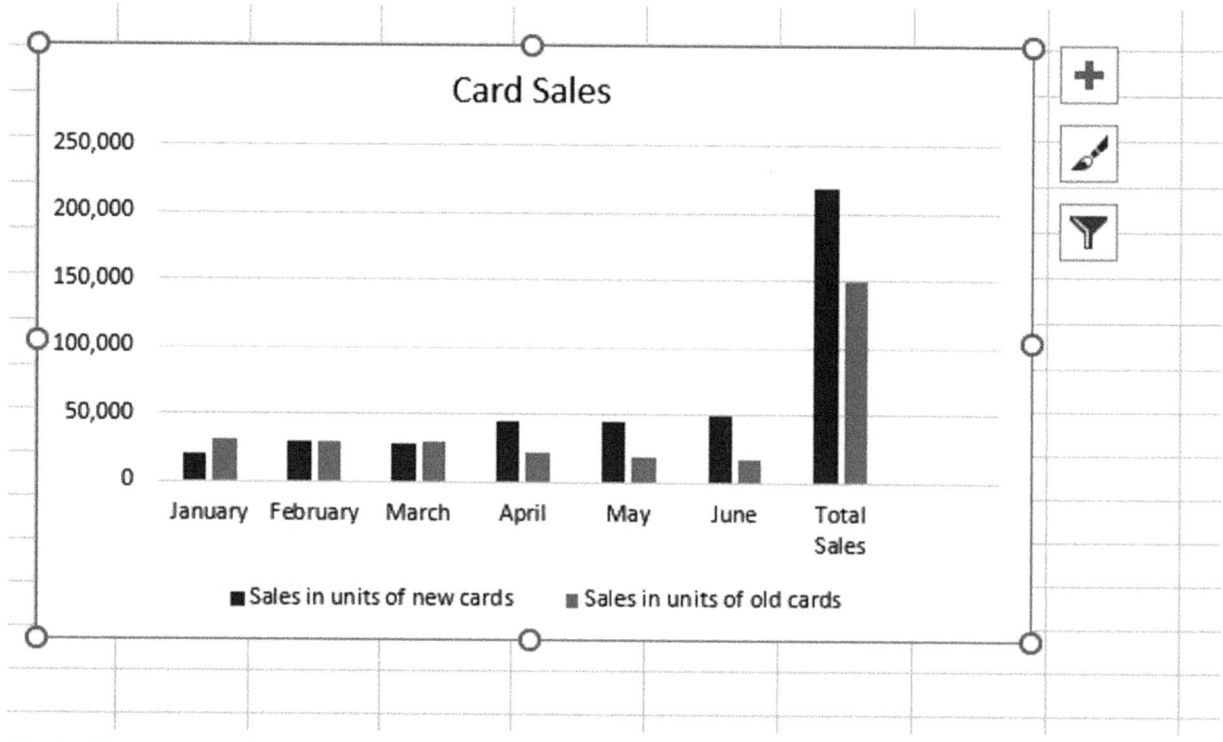

Used with permission from Microsoft.

If you wish to change the colours or anything else, use the buttons to the side of the chart. The top button allows you to change labels or add other features.

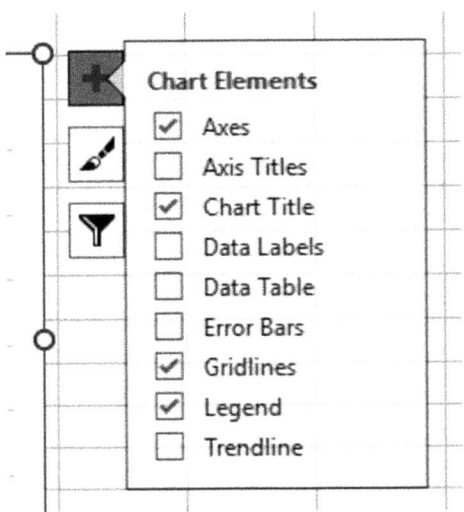

Used with permission from Microsoft.

The second button allows you to revisit the chart style option, but also lets you select alternative colours for your diagram.

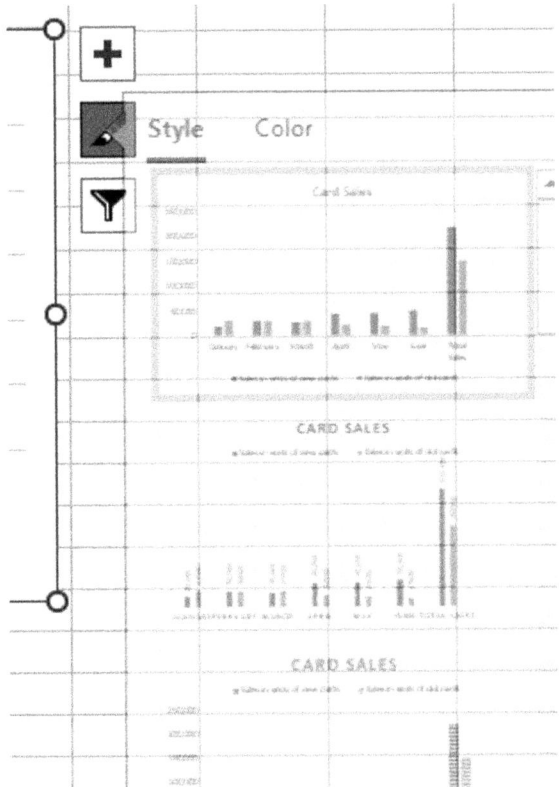

Used with permission from Microsoft.

The third button is a bit more sophisticated, and allows you to change or edit the data series and specific unit labels.

Well now you have read this, have a go!

Chapter 12
Answers to practice questions

Chapter 1

Practice questions 1

1. (a) 40
   (b) 60
   (c) 70
   (d) 90

2. (a) 400
   (b) 500
   (c) 200
   (d) 300

3. (a) 4,000
   (b) 47,000
   (c) 5,000
   (d) 7,000

4. (a) 3,000,000
   (b) 8,000,000
   (c) 10,000,000
   (d) 11,000,000

Practice questions 2

(a)	(b)	(c)	(d)	Total
964	17,201	369	639	19,173
328	34	482	1,291	2,135
792	931	79	421	2,223
236	1,074	3,121	829	5,260
2,320	19,240	4,051	3,180	28,791
				Grand total

Practice questions 3

(a)
```
  349
 −271
  ───
   78
```

(b)
```
  924
 −716
  ───
  208
```

(c)
```
 1,126
 − 379
  ───
   747
```

Practice questions 4

(a)
```
    743
 ×   21
   ────
 15,603
```

(b)
```
    641
 ×   39
   ────
 24,999
```

(c)
```
   3,216
 ×   254
  ─────
 816,864
```

Practice questions 5

(a) $1,581 \div 17 = 93$
(b) $15,792 \div 21 = 752$
(c) $139,584 \div 16 = 8,724$

Practice questions 6

(a) $5 + (-1) = 4$
(b) $(-8) + 15 = 7$
(c) $7 - (-5) = 12$
(d) $13 + (-17) = -4$
(e) $(-16) + 4 = -12$
(f) $(-14) - (-3) = -11$
(g) $(-9) + (-6) = -15$

Practice questions 7

(a) $(7 + 4) \times 3 + 2$
$= 11 \times 3 + 2$
$= 33 + 2$
$= 35$

(b) $(7 + 4) \times (3 + 7)$
$= 11 \times 10$
$= 110$

(c) $14 \times (6 + 3) - (15 \div 3)$
$= 14 \times 9 - 5$
$= 126 - 5$
$= 121$

(d) $36 + 36 \div (3 \times 1)$
$= 36 + 36 \div 3$
$= 36 + 12$
$= 48$

(e) $7 \times (48 \div [2 \times 2])$
$= 7 \times (48 \div 4)$
$= 7 \times 12$
$= 84$

(f) $(16 \div [3 + 1] + 8 + [3 \times 1] \times 6) \div 5$
$= (16 \div 4 + 8 + 3 \times 6) \div 5$
$= (4 + 8 + 18) \div 5$
$= 30 \div 5$
$= 6$

Chapter 2

Practice questions 1

(a) $1\frac{6}{7}$

(b) $3\frac{1}{6}$

(c) $7\frac{1}{4}$

(d) $4\frac{1}{8}$

(e) $7\frac{5}{6}$

Practice questions 2

(a) $\frac{22}{3}$

(b) $\frac{58}{9}$

(c) $\frac{31}{4}$

(d) $\frac{47}{9}$

Practice questions 3

(a) $\frac{1}{3}$

(b) $\frac{2}{3}$

(c) $\frac{1}{8}$

(d) $\frac{1}{3}$

(e) $\frac{1}{5}$

(f) $\frac{1}{3}$

(g) $\frac{1}{5}$

Practice questions 4

(a) $\frac{4}{12}$

(b) $\frac{12}{30}$

(c) $\frac{9}{27}$

(d) $\frac{49}{77}$

Practice questions 5

(a) $\frac{1}{2} + \frac{1}{6}$

$= \frac{3}{6} + \frac{1}{6}$

$= \frac{4}{6} = \frac{2}{3}$

(b) $\frac{1}{3} + \frac{1}{9}$

$= \frac{3}{9} + \frac{1}{9}$

$= \frac{4}{9}$

(c) $\frac{1}{5} + \frac{7}{8}$

$= \frac{8}{40} + \frac{35}{40}$

$= \frac{43}{40}$

$= 1\frac{3}{40}$

(d) $\frac{2}{6} + \frac{9}{12}$

$= \frac{4}{12} + \frac{9}{12}$

$= \frac{13}{12}$

$= 1\frac{1}{12}$

(e) $\frac{3}{4} - \frac{1}{5}$

$= \frac{15}{20} - \frac{4}{20}$

$= \frac{11}{20}$

(f) $\frac{7}{8} - \frac{2}{12}$

$= \frac{7}{8} - \frac{1}{6}$

$= \frac{21}{24} - \frac{4}{24}$

$= \frac{17}{24}$

(g) $\frac{5}{6} - \frac{4}{9}$

$= \frac{45}{54} - \frac{24}{54}$

$= \frac{21}{54}$

$= \frac{7}{18}$

(h) $\frac{6}{7} - \frac{1}{3}$

$= \frac{18}{21} - \frac{7}{21}$

$= \frac{11}{21}$

(i) $2\frac{3}{4} + 4\frac{1}{2}$

$= (2 + 4) + (\frac{3}{4} + \frac{1}{2})$

$= 6 + (\frac{3}{4} + \frac{2}{4})$

$= 6 + \frac{5}{4}$

$= 6 + 1\frac{1}{4}$

$= 7\frac{1}{4}$

(j) $6\frac{7}{8} + 7\frac{1}{16}$

$= (6 + 7) + (\frac{7}{8} + \frac{1}{16})$

$= 13 + (\frac{14}{16} + \frac{1}{16})$

$= 13\frac{15}{16}$

(k) $7\frac{2}{5} - 4\frac{1}{10}$

$= (7 - 4) + (\frac{2}{5} - \frac{1}{10})$

$= 3 + (\frac{4}{10} - \frac{1}{10})$

$= 3 + \frac{3}{10}$

$= 3\frac{3}{10}$

(l) $4\frac{1}{2} + 6\frac{3}{4} - 2\frac{1}{8}$

$= (4 + 6 - 2) + (\frac{1}{2} + \frac{3}{4} - \frac{1}{8})$

$= (10 - 2) + (\frac{4}{8} + \frac{6}{8} - \frac{1}{8})$

$= 8 + \frac{9}{8}$

$= 8 + 1\frac{1}{8}$

$= 9\frac{1}{8}$

(m) $7\frac{3}{8} + 7\frac{2}{6} - 1\frac{8}{9}$

$= (7 + 7 - 1) + (\frac{3}{8} + \frac{2}{6} - \frac{8}{9})$

$= 13 + (\frac{27}{72} + \frac{24}{72} - \frac{64}{72})$

$= 13 + (-\frac{13}{72})$

$= 13 - \frac{13}{72}$

$= 12\frac{59}{72}$

Practice questions 6

(a) $9 \times \frac{2}{5}$

$= \frac{18}{5}$

$= 3\frac{3}{5}$

(b) $18 \times \frac{1}{6}$

$= \frac{18}{6}$

$= 3$

(c) $23 \times \frac{2}{9}$

$= \frac{46}{9}$

$= 5\frac{1}{9}$

(d) $\frac{11}{33} \div 7$

$= \frac{11}{231}$

$= \frac{1}{21}$

(e) $\frac{6}{11} \div 4$

$= \frac{6}{44}$

$= \frac{3}{22}$

(f) $\frac{17}{19} \div 6$

$= \frac{17}{114}$

Practice questions 7

(a) $\frac{3}{4} \times \frac{2}{3}$

$= \frac{3 \times 2}{4 \times 3}$

$= \frac{6}{12}$

$= \frac{1}{2}$

(b) $\frac{3}{6} \times \frac{5}{7}$

$= \frac{3 \times 5}{6 \times 7}$

$= \frac{15}{42}$

$= \frac{5}{14}$

(c) $\frac{4}{7} \times \frac{6}{9}$

$= \frac{4 \times 6}{7 \times 9}$

$= \frac{24}{63}$

$= \frac{8}{21}$

(d) $\frac{6}{11} \times \frac{5}{7}$

$= \frac{6 \times 5}{11 \times 7}$

$= \frac{30}{77}$

Practice questions 8

(a) $4 \div \frac{3}{4}$

$= 4 \times \frac{4}{3}$

$= \frac{16}{3}$

$= 5\frac{1}{3}$

(b) $\frac{1}{8} \div \frac{1}{4}$

$= \frac{1}{8} \times \frac{4}{1}$

$= \frac{4}{8}$

$= \frac{1}{2}$

(c) $\frac{1}{7} \div \frac{1}{14}$

$= \frac{1}{7} \times \frac{14}{1}$

$= \frac{14}{7} = 2$

(d) $\frac{1}{6} \div \frac{1}{2}$

$= \frac{1}{6} \times \frac{2}{1}$

$= \frac{2}{6}$

$= \frac{1}{3}$

Chapter 3

Practice questions 1

(a) 7/10
(b) 17/20
(c) 81/100
(d) 901/2,000

Practice questions 2

(a) 0.009
(b) 0.003
(c) 0.026
(d) 0.709

Practice questions 3

(a) 0.04
(b) 0.12
(c) 0.15625
(d) 0.90769…
(e) 1.625

Practice questions 4

Add up ratios: 4 + 5 + 6 = 15

Alpha	4/15 × $450,000 = $120,000
Beta	5/15 × $450,000 = $150,000
Omega	6/15 × $450,000 = $180,000

Practice questions 5

(a) 15/25 = 0.6 = 60%
(b) 5/11 = 0.45 = 45%
(c) 36/40 = 0.90 = 90%

Practice questions 6

(a) 31.25
(b) 297
(c) 60
(d) 16.2

Practice questions 7

(a) 50%
(b) 25%
(c) 57%
(d) 170%

Practice questions 8

(a) 41.7%
(b) 40%
(c) 44%

Practice questions 9

(a) 102
(b) 517.5
(c) 72
(d) 280
(e) 4,680

Chapter 5

Practice questions 1

(a) Anne's earnings

Week 1	
35 hours × £15 per hour	£525.00
3 hours × (£15 × 1.5)	£67.50
Total week 1	£592.50
Week 2	
35 hours × £15 per hour	£525.00
6 hours × (£15 × 1.5)	£135.00
Total week 2	£660.00
Total earnings for 2 weeks	£1,252.50

(b) With Saturdays
Previous earnings £1,252.50
Saturdays' earnings (14 hours × £15 × 2) £420.00
£1,672.50

(c) Bob's earnings
Week 1
35 hours × £11 per hour £385
8 hours × (£11 × 1.5) £132
2 hours × (£11 × 2) £44
Total week 1 £561

Week 2
35 hours × £11 per hour £385
10 hours × (£11 × 1.5) £165
6 hours × (£11 × 2) £132
Total week 2 £682

Total earnings for 2 weeks £1,243

(d) Anita's earnings
Week 1
40 hours × £15 per hour £600.00
3 hours × £22.50 £67.50
2 hours × £30 £60.00
Total week 1 £727.50

Week 2
40 hours × £15 per hour £600.00
4 hours × £22.50 £90.00
4 hours × £30 £120.00
Total week 2 £810.00

Total earnings for 2 weeks £1,537.50

Practice question 2

Earnings £36,000
Less Personal allowance £11,500
Taxable pay £24,500

Tax liability: 25% × £24,500 = £6,125

Total earnings after tax: £36,000 − £6,125 = £29,875

Monthly salary is £29,875 ÷ 12 = £2,489.58 per month

Practice questions 3

		VAT @ 25%	Selling price including VAT
Item 1	£250	£62.50	£312.50
Item 2	£930	£232.50	£1,162.50
Item 3	£650	£162.50	£812.50
Item 4	£1,220	£305	£1,525

Practice question 4

Initial capital cost of machine   £250,000
Value at the end of 4 years   £10,000
Amount to be depreciated in 4 years   £240,000

Depreciation per year is £240,000 ÷ 4 = £60,000 per year

Practice question 5

Sigma's salary would be £69,000
Omega's salary would be 0.5% of £5 million (£25,000), plus 0.75% of 5 million (£37,500) = £62,500
Therefore, Sigma offers the better salary if sales are exactly £10 million.

Practice questions 6

Item	Discount offered	Original price	Discount	Selling price
A	10%	£600	£60	£540
B	18%	£200	£36	£164
C	12.5%	£800	£100	£700
D	16%	£90	£14.40	£75.60
E	33%	£300	£99	£201

Chapter 6

Practice questions 1

(a) Principal   £6,000
    Interest at 3.5% p.a. (£210 p.a. × 3)   £630
    Total paid back   £6,630

(b) Interest at 2% of £10,000   £200
    Interest for 5 years   £1,000

Practice question 2

Principal	£15,000.00
Year 1 interest 4% × £15,000	£600.00
Amount owed at end of Year 1	£15,600.00
Year 2 interest 4% × £15,600	£624.00
	£16,224.00
Year 3 interest 4% × £16,224	£648.96
	£16,872.96
Year 4 interest 4% × £16,872.96	£674.92
Amount repayable	£17,547.88

Practice questions 3

(a)
Amount	£80,000
Interest at 6% = £480 p.a.	
Interest at end of year 4	£19,200
Total	£99,200

(b)
Principal	£80,000
Year 1 interest 8% × £80,000	£6,400
	£86,400
Year 2 interest 8% × £86,400	£6,912
	£93,312
Year 3 interest 8% × £93,312	£7,465
	£100,777
Year 4 interest 8% × £100,777	£8,062
Amount repayable	£108,839

Practice questions 4

(a)
Principal	£30,000
Year 1 interest 7% × £30,000	£2,100
Amount in account at end of Year 1	£32,100
Year 2 interest 7% × £32,100	£2,247
Amount in account at end of Year 2	£34,347
Year 3 interest 7% × £34,347	£2,404.29
Total in account at end of Year 3	£36,751.29

(b) Business investment £30,000
Year 1 income £9,500
Year 2 income £11,500
Year 3 income £13,000
Total £64,000

Therefore, the alternative business investment is the better option.

Practice questions 5

(a) In 2018   300,000 ÷ 1.31 = £229,007.63
(b) In 2019   300,000 ÷ 1.16 = £258,620.68
(c) Exchange rates: 2018   1.31
                      2019   −1.16
                             0.15

Depreciation = (0.15 ÷ 1.31) × 100 = 11.45%

Practice questions 6

(a) 300 × €1.38 = €414
    Total cost = 414 ÷ 1.17 = £353.85
(b) Cost per litre in pence = 1.38 ÷ 1.17 = 118 pence (rounded)

Chapter 8

Practice question 1

Month	Sales in units
January	20,000
February	30,000
March	28,000
April	45,000
May	46,000
June	50,000

Source: Sales manager
Table of monthly sales

A total could also be provided, i.e. 219,000

Practice question 2

Month	Sales in units	Percentage of sales
January	20,000	9.13%
February	30,000	13.70%
March	28,000	12.79%
April	45,000	20.55%
May	46,000	21.00%
June	50,000	22.83%

Source: Sales manager
Table of monthly sales of new card range in units with total and percentage share of sales

Practice question 3

Month	Sales in units of new cards	Percentage of sales of new cards	Sales in units of old cards	Percentage of sales of old cards
January	20,000	9.13%	31,500	20.93%
February	30,000	13.70%	30,000	19.93%
March	28,000	12.79%	29,900	19.87%
April	45,000	20.55%	22,500	14.95%
May	46,000	21.00%	19,600	13.02%
June	50,000	22.83%	17,000	11.30%
Total sales	219,000	100%	150,500	100%

Source: Card company accounts
Table of monthly sales of new and old card ranges in units with total and percentage share of sales

While month by month the sales of the new cards are increasing the old card range is declining. Most notable is the percentage change in how important sales are to each card type between the beginning of the period and by the end of the period.

Practice question 4

The first step is the totals, the second is the calculation of the percentages.

Year	Quarter	Total sales	Vere Sales	Aldhere Sales	Vere Sales	Aldhere Sales
		£000	£000	£000	%	%
2017	1	4,500	3,200	1,300	71.1	28.9
	2	4,600	3,180	1,420	69.1	30.9
	3	4,700	3,020	1,680	64.3	35.7
	4	4,750	3,000	1,750	63.2	36.8
2018	1	4,800	2,900	1,900	60.4	39.6
	2	4,850	2,950	1,900	60.8	39.2
	3	4,875	2,950	1,925	60.5	39.5
	4	4,900	2,950	1,950	60.2	39.8
Total		37,975	24,150	13,825		

Source: Company sales

Table of sales of sterile bandages

This table tells the user that Vere is the more important product in terms of total sales. However, it also illustrates the growth of Aldhere at the expense of Vere's declining sales over the two years. The decision on which product, if any, to axe is not an easy one. Vere is the better selling product, but it is declining in sales while Aldhere's are rising. It is, indeed, a difficult decision that you are not being asked to make!

Practice question 5

There are a variety of different ways to present this data. Here are a few alternatives.

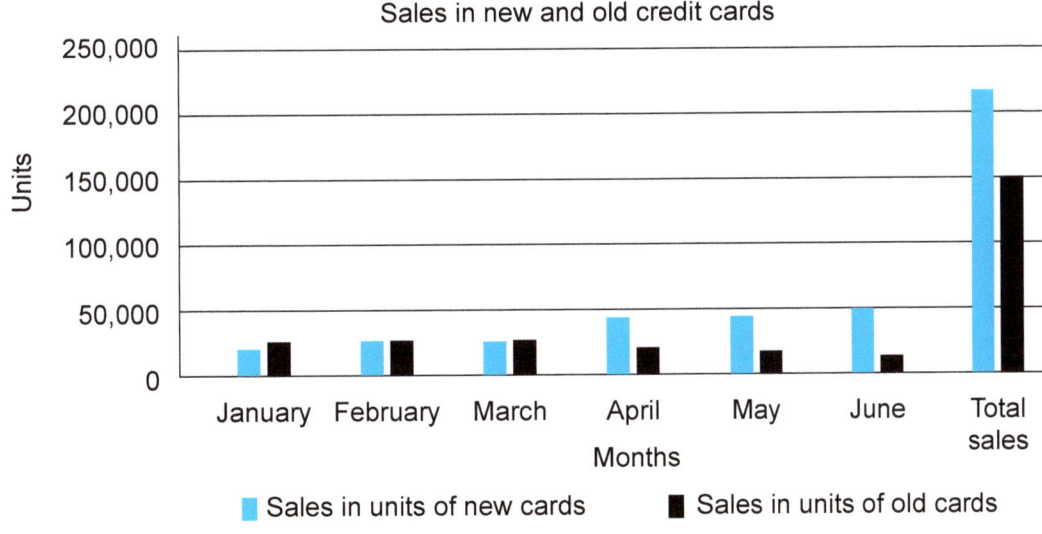

Practice question 3

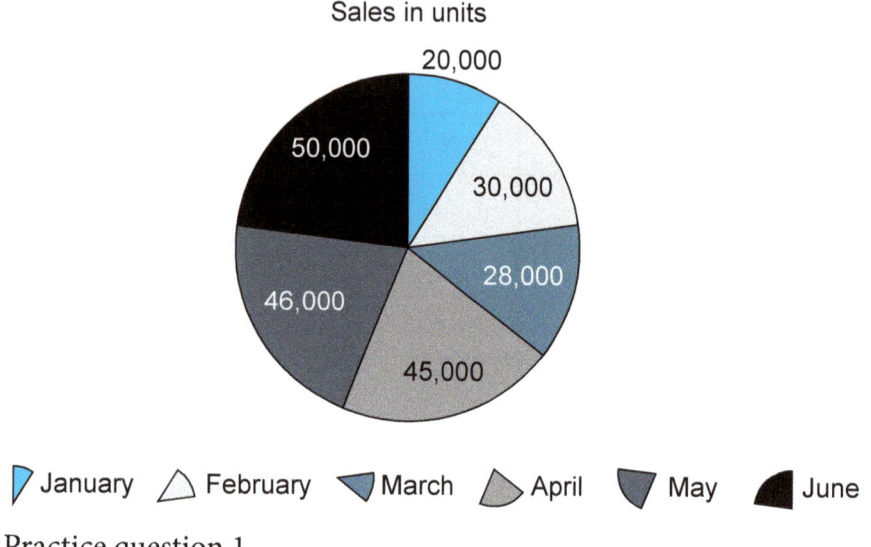

Practice question 1

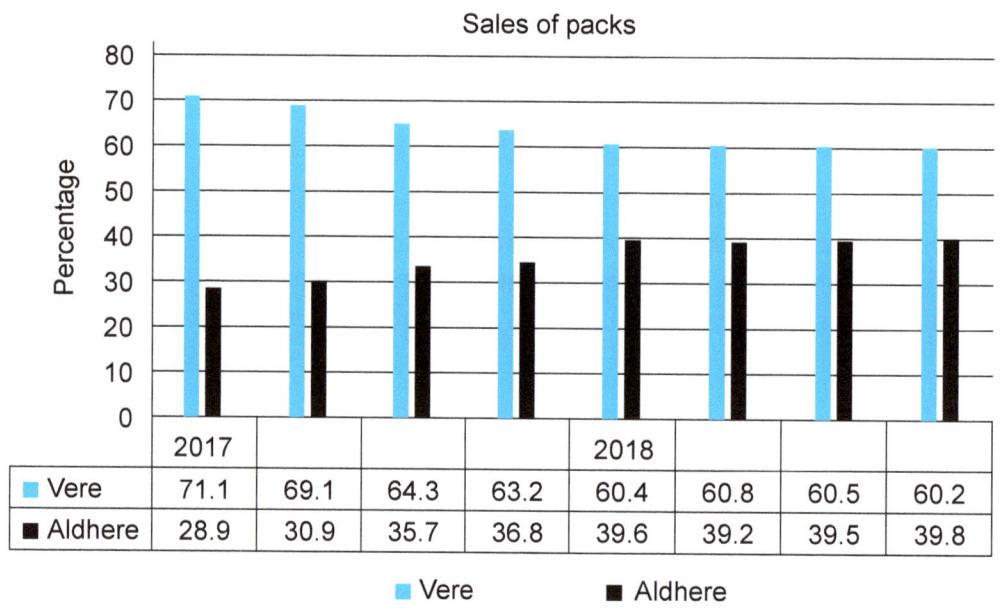

Practice question 4

Chapter 9

Practice question 1

Customer interactions	Tally	Frequency
3	/	1
5	//	2
6	///	3
9	/	1
12	////	4
14	///	3
15	///	3
16	////	5
17	///	3
18	////	4
19	//	2
20	/	1
21	/	1
22	///	3
23	/	1
24	//	2
25	/	1
Total frequency		40

Tally and frequency table

It is hard to discern much from this table except where some of the bunching is and a clearer picture of the extremes. Further analysis is needed. This could be an alternative representation such as the chart overleaf or the calculation of the mean, see later in the chapter.

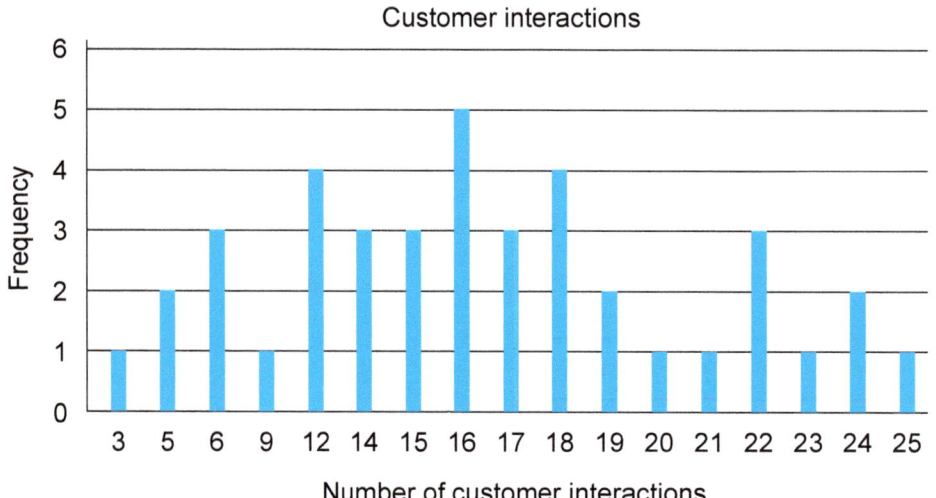

Practice question 2

The mode is 12.3 kgs

Practice question 3

The median is 13 kgs

Practice question 4

The mean is 12.95 kgs

Practice question 5

Mean	15.475
Mode	16
Median	16

www.ingramcontent.com/pod-product-compliance
Ingram Content Group UK Ltd.
Pitfield, Milton Keynes, MK11 3LW, UK
UKHW050033281125
465503UK00001B/1